READING'S MOVIE MEMORIES

250th Anniversary Edition

Barbara A. Wade
P.O. Box 29
Newmanstown, PA 17073

Design by Hash-Heffner Graphics, Gretchen Hash-Heffner

ISBN 0-9658505-0-1

Dedicated to Paul E. Glase, whose voluminous theatre
collection and writings made this book possible,
and
to my Mother, Mary Heft, who allowed me to be
a "movie kid."
May they both be "smiling down" on this project.

Other Books by Barbara A. Wade

Memories of a City - Reading in the 40's and 50's
Remembrances of Reading

Contents:

About the Author

Barbara A. Wade is a graduate of Kutztown State College, now Kutztown University, where she earned a B.S. in Education and an M.A. in English. Although she was born in Reading, PA, and resided in Berks County for close to sixty years, she now lives in Lebanon County. However, her fondest memories are of growing up in Reading in the forties and fifties when movie theatres dotted its main street. This is her tribute to those film palaces.

Acknowledgments

First and foremost, I owe a great debt of gratitude to John Glase, Paul E. Glase's grandson, who was kind enough to share some of his grandfather's collection with me. Paul Glase, or "Peg" as he was known to his friends, died on September 22, 1955, leaving behind a theatrical heritage of more than thirty scrapbooks and thousands of programs and photographs illustrating the history of entertainment in Reading. This theatrical history, which reached back to the late eighteenth century, was later condensed in a series of articles written from 1946 to 1948 for publication in the *Historical Review of Berks County*. Without Mr. Glase's foresight, Reading and Berks County would have little record of the area's rich theatrical heritage. I must also thank the Historical Society of Berks County, particularly Barbara Gill, for allowing me to peruse Peg Glase's scrapbooks which are now in the society's archives. Gratitude is also owed to Charles M. Gallagher, managing editor of the *Reading Eagle/Times*, who approved the use of the local papers' photos, ads, and articles dealing with Reading's movie theatres over the last century. Appreciation is expressed to Ron Romanski, Ira Bergman, Donald Mellinger, Dixie Kreider, George M. Meiser, IX, and the late Richard Houck for sharing information and photos with me. I am grateful to Frank McGough for allowing me to copy movie theatre photos from the files of the Reading Redevelopment Authority. Thanks to Jean Lawrence and Oliver Epler who supplied me with the dates of the Zerbe Hardware fire (the old Rio Theatre), and, finally, many thanks to the former employees of Reading's film houses for sharing their photos and fond memories. These include Ed Foley, Eugene Deeter, William Richter, Vera (Reidel) Wennell, and my friend, Elmer Quinn, who went out of his way to help me with this project. To anyone else who may have contributed to this book, I extend heartfelt appreciation.

Author's Notes

Much of the information in this book comes from the collections and writings of Paul E. Glase (particularly material dealing with the beginning years to 1948), the *Reading Eagle and Reading Times*, and the recollections of people who worked in Reading's theatres or loved attending them. The latter category includes the author. This volume is by no means a definitive work on this area's movie theatres. Rather, it is a labor of love by one who spent many pleasant hours sitting in the darkened auditoriums of these movie palaces whose elegance and splendor were reason enough for buying a ticket. In the days of these theatres, "going to the movies" was an exciting and richly rewarding experience.

I have focused on the theatres that I remember and attended. Certainly, some of you will have memories of other theatres that are not included in this book. For those who wish to explore these other movie houses, or for those who wish to do more in-depth reading on the subject, I refer you to the source material page of this volume. In addition, readers will find that some theatres are covered more extensively than others. Be assured that this is not due to any prejudice on my part but, rather, to the availability of information on a particular movie house. Likewise, photographs of some theatres were difficult to find; therefore, some theatre sections carry only one photograph. In the case of the Rio, no photographs could be found, so a computer sketch by John Wade was used. I hope it comes close to resembling that little theatre on Schuylkill Avenue. Also, movie ads appear in the book because they were artistic creations unto themselves and played a large part in enticing people to come to the movies. Today, whole pages of illustrated film ads in the daily newspapers are rare.

It is hoped that this volume will take you back to those movie palace days when the films, and the theatres in which they were shown, possessed both style and class. So now that you have your ticket, grab that box of jujubes, sit back in that red velvet seat, and let's go to the movies!

Theatre advertising on Reading's trolley cars. Photo courtesy of John Glase.

READING'S MOVIE MEMORIES

250th Anniversary Edition

OUR EARLIEST MOVIE HOUSES

At top from left - PICTURELAND, 645 Penn St.; THE STAR (formerly LIBERTY), 547 Penn St.; THE CRESCENT, 819 Penn St.; Lower from left, THE EMPIRE, 739 Penn St.; THE FIRST VICTOR, 732 Penn St.; THE MECCA, 717 Penn St. Photos from Paul E. Glase's *Annals of the Reading Theatre - 1791-1948.* Courtesy of John Glase of Kenhorst.

1. Some Beginnings

According to Paul E. Glase's *Annals of the Reading Theatre*, the first established site in Reading where motion pictures were shown consecutively was on the northeast corner of 3rd and Penn. This marvelous feat occurred in the summer of 1899 when a projector was set up on the third floor of a hotel on the northwest corner and the images projected onto a canvas stretched across the building on the opposite side. As there was no automobile traffic, crowds could gather safely on the pavement and street to watch the short comic subjects and the local business advertisements while sampling colored, flavored ice sold from an express wagon by one of Reading's young entrepreneurs. Of course, these early enterprising projectionists could not have imagined that, for the next fifty years, Reading would become home to numerous movie palaces through whose brass-trimmed doors thousands would flock daily to see the latest Hollywood fantasies.

Glase relates that there were many attempts to establish motion picture houses in Reading during the early part of the twentieth century. The first motion picture theatre in this city was the Electric Theatre, which opened in 1905 at 411 Penn Street in a portion of the Old Central House, later to house the Acme Market. Presently, CNA Insurance occupies the site. This first theatre later became the People's Theatre. Also, in those days, Thomas Harford was exhibiting pictures at Carsonia Park in the Mirror Maze, a small nickelodeon with ninety folding chairs. Also operating at Carsonia at this time was the Carsonia Park Theatre under the management of Lee Lamar, and, later, Cook and Harford.

The first Victor Theatre was opened in 1906 by Rothleter and Schwalin in the lower section of the old Bijou building at 736 Penn Street, later the site of the Astor Theatre. Since it occupied space between a poolroom and the Bijou lobby entrance, the Victor's width was limited to fifteen feet and its seating to 142 patrons. Nevertheless, the tiny movie house played an important part in the history of the motion picture theatre in Reading as it was later purchased by Carr and Schad, two of the major operators of movie theatres in this city.

In his theatrical history articles, Mr. Glase relates that Claude L. Carr and Harry J. Schad met at Carsonia Park where Mr. Schad ran a soda stand on weekends. During the week, Schad conducted a drug store at 122 North Fifth Street while Carr was an agent for display showroom cases. Their meeting at Carsonia Park resulted in a partnership whose first venture was the operation of the park's carousel. Then, in 1907, the pair purchased the Victor Theatre as their first movie house enterprise. In 1909, the duo opened the "new" Victor at 748 Penn Street. Glase recalls that this newest Carr and Schad film house contained many innovations in theatre building, including a mirrored lobby and a brilliantly-lighted entrance.

One of the city's best known early picture houses, Pictureland, was opened in 1909 by George Bennethun at 645 Penn Street, and it was here that the first mirror screen was introduced, along with the first orchestra in a local movie house. Elmer Quinn of Reading, who was a projectionist and orchestra musician in various theatres, recalls that Pictureland contained rows of four seats on each side of the aisle and an electric piano whose music never matched the action on the screen. It was at Pictureland that Bertrand Mellinger, chief projectionist at the Loew's Colonial for many years, began his career in 1916 at $10 a week. According to his son, Donald, Mellinger worked six days a week, Monday through Saturday, with a one hour break for supper. In those early days of the cinema, there were ten shows a day, each one hour long, with films changing daily. Mellinger also worked at the Gem and the Hippodrome before moving to the Loew's. Margaret Maty, a patron of Pictureland, also recalled some memories of the old theatre in an article written by Shirley Shirey for the April 4, 1968, edition of the *Berks County Record*. In the article, entitled "Reading's Old-Time Picture Houses Revisited," Maty remembers that the interior of the picture house always smelled of tobacco juice which the male patrons would

The Hippodrome at 753 Penn Street, later to become the State and, in 1941, the Warner. Photo courtesy of John Glase.

spit on the floor. In addition, she recalls that the younger members of the audience would shoot peas at the piano player, an action which further hindered the musician's ability to synchronize the music with the film.

Also in 1909, Ben Zerr and Francis Stetler opened the Empire Theatre at 739 Penn Street (later the location of the Embassy Bar) which was purchased in 1912 by Carr and Schad. This theatre partnership also purchased the Lyric which had been built by Theodore Auman, J. George Kuersten, J. George Rick, and Frank D. Hill in 1910 at 808 - 810 Penn Street. This motion picture house was unique in that its steps ran the entire length of the building, raising the box office six feet above the sidewalk. Another significant event occurred on July 4, 1914, when the Lyric dedicated the "Mammoth Moller Pipe Organ," the first of its kind to be used in Reading. Tragically, in 1925, three years after Carr and Schad purchased the building, it was destroyed by fire, never to reopen.

Of interest is the fact that in 1922 a company called Reading Screen Service attempted to turn back the clock by placing a screen on the wall of a building on the northeast corner of 7th and Penn (later Read's Department Store) and a projection booth in a top window of the Hotel Allen on the northwest corner. Fortunately, the location was a handicap, especially since the railroad tracks intervened, and the operation was discontinued. However, Reading was to have many motion picture houses in which to fulfill its citizens' celluloid dreams.

The Lyric Theatre at 808-810 Penn Street. Notice the large ad for Moller's Mammoth Pipe Organ. The Lyric was destroyed by fire in 1925.
Photo courtesy of John Glase.

FRANKLIN THEATRE NEWS

"Judgement of the Hills" with Virginia Valli and Frankie Darro

Coming to Arcadia

All the stark [illegible] of the Kentucky mountaineers is brought to the screen in "Judgment of the Hills," the remarkable F. B. O. picture which comes to the Arcadia theatre week of Feb. 27.

It is this atmosphere of the uncouth hillsmen that is perhaps the most unusual feature of the production, and which has helped to make it one of the outstanding motion pictures of the year. Director Leo Meehan is said to have maintained an illusion of reality which is in every way remarkable, and he was fortunate in having the services of a cast which has done full justice to the story.

The lovely Virginia Valli plays the leading feminine role, that of a gently-reared school teacher who goes to Grayson's Gap to take charge of the education of the children in this rude mountain community. The role of the "hero" — (who is decidedly not a hero)—is in the hands of Orville Caldwell, who achieved fame for his playing of 'The Knight' in Morris Gest's great stage production, "The Miracle." The part of Tad Dennison, the third of the leading characters in "Judgement of the Hills" is played by eight year old Frankie Darro, hailed as the logical successor to Jackie Coogan.

SCHUYLKILL AVE. THEATRE

(Sch. Ave. and Oley Sts.)
SATURDAY NIGHT ONLY
February 25th, 1928
RICHARD TALMADGE
The Screen's foremost action star in
"THE BETTER MAN"
A Leaping, Whirling Action Drama

Comedy, "Heavy Hikers"

HAYDEN STEVENSON in the 3rd Chapter
"Blake of Scotland Yard"

ROYAL
Church & Spring Sts

MONDAY and TUESDAY
Warner Bros. presents
"THE PASSIONATE QUEST"
A drama of the theatre, big business and romance
Starring May McAvoy
Willard Louis, Louise Fazenda
Comedy, "Keeping Her Wed"

WEDNESDAY
"SNOWBOUND"
Hemmed in by a raging blizzard there was no escape and love finally conquered.
Cast Includes
Betty Blythe, Lillian Rich and Robert Agnew
Comedy
"The Wrong Mrs. Wright"

THURSDAY and FRIDAY
Carl Laemmle presents
BILLIE DOVE and HUNTLEY GORDON in
"SENSATION SEEKERS"
From the story "Egypt" by Ernest Pascal.
3rd CHAPTER
"Blake of Scotland Yard"

SATURDAY
TOM TYLER
and his "Pals" in
SPLITTING THE BREEZE

RIVOLI
Laurel nr 6th St.

MONDAY and TUESDAY
"TWO GIRLS WANTED"
A story of love, romance and thrills—Starring
JANET GAYNOR
(The Sensational Star of "7th Heaven") with Ben Bard and Glenn Tryon. Glenn Tryon is the former Reading Boy).
Comedy, "George's in Love"

WEDNESDAY
Metro-Goldwyn presents
"A LITTLE JOURNEY"
Three thousand miles of love and laughter based on the play by Rachel Crothers. Cast includes Claire Windsor, William Haines, Harry Carey
Comedy, 'Some More Excuses'

THURSDAY and FRIDAY
First National presents
MILTON SILLS
with Molly O'Day in
"HARD BOILED HAGGERTY"
Taken from 'Belated Evidence'
2nd CHAPTER
"Blake of Scotland Yard"

SATURDAY
ART ACORD
In a Blue Streak Western
"HARD FISTS"
Comedy, "Old Tin Sides"

VICTORIA
Moss & Exeter Sts

MONDAY and TUESDAY
Warner Bros. present
"FOOTLOOSE WIDOWS"
A love story of the Florida Beaches—Introducing
LOUISE FAZENDA and
JACQUELINE LOGAN
Comedy, "Peaceful Oscar"

WEDNESDAY
Metro-Goldwyn presents
"CALIFORNIA"
By Peter B. Kyne.
Starring the popular Western Star, TIM McCOY
Comedy 'Love 'Em and Weep'

THURSDAY and FRIDAY
Carl Laemmle presents
LAURA LA PLANTE
with TOM MOORE
In a romantic thriller
"THE LOVE THRILL"
2nd CHAPTER
"Blake of Scotland Yard"

SATURDAY
TOM TYLER
and His Pals in
"CYCLONE OF THE RANGE"
Comedy, "Winnie Steps Out"

SAVOY
10th & Greenwich Sts

MONDAY and TUESDAY
Carl Laemmle presents
"THE WRONG MR. WRIGHT"
The heart breaking romance of a corset king.
The Cast Includes
JEAN HERSHOLT
Enid Bennett, Walter Hiers
Comedy, "Jane's Hubby"

WEDNESDAY
FRANK MERRILL
the world's champion athlete
—IN—
"DASHING THRU"
A tempest of thrills—A tornado of action.
Comedy, "Parcel Post"

THURSDAY and FRIDAY
F. B. O. presents
Laura Jean Libbey's Famous Story
"A POOR GIRL'S ROMANCE"
Introducing Gertrude Short and Creighton Hale
3rd CHAPTER
"Blake of Scotland Yard"

SATURDAY
TED WELLS
In a Blue Streak Western
"DESERT DUST"
Comedy, "Foiled"

Early theatre ads.
Courtesy of Elmer Quinn of Reading.

2. The Talkies Come to Reading

Glase's writings reveal that a special program took place at the Academy of Music on North 6th Street on October 1, 2, and 3, 1913, which showcased what was then regarded as the most improved of all phonographic recordings, Kinetophone. This display, which was heralded in local newspapers by the spectacular claim, "They laugh, talk, sing, and dance," included a woman playing the violin, an actress singing, and "sundry dogs barking." What a thrill this exhibition must have been for those lucky enough to secure seats at this first program of sound pictures in Reading! However, this was only the beginning of a motion picture miracle that would have Readingites flocking to their local film palaces in the near future to enjoy sophisticated sound.

On November 9 and 10, 1925, another step on the road to motion picture sound occurred when the Orpheum on North 5th Street exhibited the DeForest Phonofilm, a method by which voice and sound were photographed and projected without phonographic attachment. Mr. Glase recalls that the screen fare included Eddie Cantor, the Ben Bernie Orchestra, and two Readingites - Paul Specht and his violin and Roy Smeck, "the wizard of the strings."

Then, on February 21, 1927, the premiere presentation of sound pictures in Pennsylvania occurred when Vitaphone was presented at the Arcadia on Penn Street. The feature attraction was "Don Juan," starring John Barrymore. Although there was no talking, there were plenty of spectacular sound effects like clashing swords and clinking glasses. In addition, the New York Philharmonic played the musical score which sounded so realistic that, according to Glase, many patrons believed that the orchestra was actually in the pit. Supporting the bill were five Vitaphone acts of instrumental and vocal selections. Larry Talbot and Wallace Hill, projectionists at various theatres, including the Arcadia, remembered that day well in an interview for the August 20, 1961, edition of the *Sunday Reading Eagle Magazine*. According to the pair, they looked through the projection booth that evening to a wildly applauding audience who had just witnessed the remarkable Vitaphone process of synchronizing sound from a phonograph record to a reel of film.

But the real revolution in motion pictures arrived in Reading on New Year's Eve in 1927 when Al Jolson spoke the words, "Wait a minute, you ain't heard nothin' yet!" on the screen of the Arcadia in the first "talkie," "The Jazz Singer." For three weeks, Readingites came to the Arcadia in droves to hear one of their favorite movie stars talk and sing. When the Arcadia closed its doors in May of 1928 to make way for the Astor, the Vitaphone equipment was moved to the Strand where it continued exclusively until October 28, 1928, when the Astor opened its doors. Glase notes that one of the Vitaphone attractions at the Strand that summer was the first all-talking film, "Lights of New York," which played to capacity crowds. Reading had embraced "the talkies."

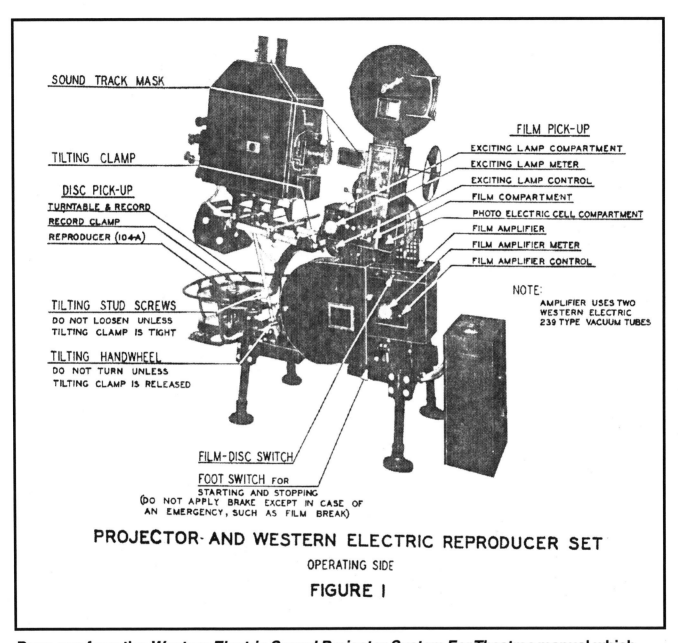

SOUND TRACK MASK

TILTING CLAMP

DISC PICK-UP
TURNTABLE & RECORD
RECORD CLAMP
REPRODUCER (104A)

TILTING STUD SCREWS
DO NOT LOOSEN UNLESS
TILTING CLAMP IS TIGHT

TILTING HANDWHEEL
DO NOT TURN UNLESS
TILTING CLAMP IS RELEASED

FILM PICK-UP
EXCITING LAMP COMPARTMENT
EXCITING LAMP METER
EXCITING LAMP CONTROL
FILM COMPARTMENT
PHOTO ELECTRIC CELL COMPARTMENT
FILM AMPLIFIER
FILM AMPLIFIER METER
FILM AMPLIFIER CONTROL

NOTE:
AMPLIFIER USES TWO
WESTERN ELECTRIC
239 TYPE VACUUM TUBES

FILM-DISC SWITCH
FOOT SWITCH FOR
STARTING AND STOPPING
(DO NOT APPLY BRAKE EXCEPT IN CASE OF
AN EMERGENCY, SUCH AS FILM BREAK)

PROJECTOR- AND WESTERN ELECTRIC REPRODUCER SET

OPERATING SIDE

FIGURE I

Page one from the *Western Electric Sound Projector System For Theatres* manual which
was published December 1, 1928, by Electric Research Product, Inc. of New York for projectionists who would be operating Western Electric's Simplex System.
Courtesy of Richard Zechman of Elizabethtown, Pennsylvania.

3. Neighborhood Theatres

In the days before Americans' love affair with the automobile (and before they could afford the courtship), neighborhoods were, of necessity, self-sufficient, with each neighborhood having a number of corner grocery stores, drug stores, soda fountains, shoe repair shops, etc. In addition to fulfilling people's physical needs, however, the neighborhood was depended upon for socialization and entertainment. Thus was born the neighborhood theatre.

Paul Glase's *Annals* reveals that the first of these theatres was the Olivet which was opened by Ben Zerr in 1911 at Schuylkill Avenue and Oley Streets in the northwest section of Reading. In 1913, this building became the Schuylkill Avenue Picture House and, later, in 1936, the Rio. Another early neighborhood theatre in Reading was the Gem at 10th and Spring, a building which still stands, its columned facade the only reminder of its past use. The Gem opened in 1912 as did Frank Gould's Rex at 17 1/2 and Cotton Streets and Ben Zerr's Benzer in the market house building at 10th and Chestnut. Also appearing in 1912 were the Star at 130 South 10th Street, Drexel and McKentley's Savoy at 10th and Greenwich, and the Gery Brothers' Royal at Church and Spring. In addition, Charles Snyder and W. Sensenig exhibited pictures at the Cozy on the south side of Mulberry Street in the 700 block the following year. Charles Graul's Victoria also opened in 1913 at 1600 Moss Street near the old trolley car barn. Then the year 1914 saw the birth of the Family Theatre in Red Men's Hall on the north side of Walnut Street between 8th and 9th Streets. One of the most remembered theatres also opened in 1914 - the San Toy on Front Street up the block from Richards Toy Corner. In an article written for the August 20, 1961, edition of the *Sunday Reading Eagle Magazine*, film projectionist Leroy Talbot remembers that each time a train or trolley rumbled past the building, the phonograph needle on the sound system jumped, throwing the sound out of synchronization. In fact, Talbot remarked that this happened so often that he could tell if either vehicle was running behind schedule. That same year, Mary Ernst opened the Laurel Theatre on Laurel Street near 6th in the building which presently houses the Sokols Athletic Association. This picture house later became the Palm and then the Rivoli before going out of business as a theatre. Also premiering was the Majestic at 108 Oley Street and Harry Witman's Queen on North 11th and Buttonwood Streets. Some older citizens may remember entering this theatre at the back of the screen and walking up the aisle to the seats since the building was built on a hill. The year 1920 witnessed the opening of one of Reading's best-known and beloved theatres - the Strand at 9th and Spring. Constructed by

The San Toy on Front Street. Passing trains would throw the sound out of sync.
Photo courtesy of John Glase.

C.H. Schlegel and Son and opened by Carr and Schad, the Strand billed itself as Reading's largest neighborhood theatre.

In 1926, a pair of Philadelphia entrepreneurs, Ben Amsterdam and Louis Korson, gained control of the Carr and Schad theatre circuit. The deal included the Strand, the San Toy, and the Schuylkill Avenue Picture House. Also acquired were two theatres on Penn Street, the Arcadia and the Princess. All were now operated by the Franklin Theatre Company which celebrated the transaction by bringing the production "Rose Marie" to the stage of the Strand direct from Philadelphia. Also to be continued at the Strand were the Haage Concerts, initiated by Carr and Schad. The next acquisition of the Franklin Company was the Warner circuit, which included the Queen, the Royal, the Rivoli, the Savoy, the Victoria, and the Rex, bringing to eleven the total number of theatres acquired by the company.

Unfortunately, the days of most of the neighborhood theatres were numbered for, according to Paul E. Glase, these houses had a limited seating capacity which, combined with their low scale of ticket prices, brought about their demise. With the passing of silent films in 1929, most owners could ill afford the expense of equipping their buildings for sound. Thus, most of the early neighborhood theatres passed from the scene. Sadly, they took with them a huge chunk of the neighborhood's soul.

Reading Eagle ad for May 4, 1920.

10

Some neighborhood theatre ads - *Reading Eagle* - March 1946.

4. The Strand

As mentioned in the previous section, few small neighborhood theatres could afford to make the switch to sound, so most of them quietly faded away like the silent films that had brought them into existence. However, a few managed to survive. Among these survivors was the Strand Theatre at 9th and Spring Streets in Reading.

The city's largest neighborhood theater was constructed by C.H. Schlegel and Son and opened on February 21, 1920. As the *Reading Eagle* ad of that day proclaimed, the public would now be able to see "the best attractions produced without taking the time to dress up and go downtown." A Carr and Schad theatre, the Strand contained 1,750 seats and, in its early years, featured motion pictures, vaudeville, and stage attractions. The Haage Concert Series was also moved to this theatre when the Rajah burned in 1921. On September 21, 1925, Paul Whiteman and his band opened their transcontinental tour at the Strand with vocalist Morton Downey. An ad for the theatre in the October 3, 1925, edition of the *Eagle* boasted of three performances of vaudeville and pictures featuring Dunbar and Turner in slapstick and conversation that will "make the house rock" and Buster Keaton in the feature film, "The Navigator." Even greater still was the attraction scheduled for the following week - the Mason Brothers gigantic stage play, "Uncle Tom's Cabin." The Strand's stage was also the setting for many benefit programs. Elmer Quinn remembers playing there for the Billy Levan Orchestra which was performing to raise funds for Mississippi flood relief.

On May 3, 1926, this Ninth and Spring film house, along with other theatres in the Carr and Schad chain, was taken over by Ben Amsterdam and Louis Korson. The Strand again changed hands in 1930 when Warner Brothers acquired control, continuing its operation until May 1941 when the theatre reverted to H.J. Schad who undertook a complete renovation. On May 29, 1941, Schad's Strand

> ## Announcement to Residents of Northeastern Section
>
> # STRAND THEATRE
>
> ——NINTH *and* SPRING STREETS——
>
> Opening Some Day This Week :: Watch Papers for Date
>
> ### To the Public
>
> IN giving you the Strand Theatre we have given you one of the finest photoplay theatres in the country. We want you to realise that this is your theatre, and that you will be able to see the best attractions produced without taking the time and trouble to "dress up" and go down town.
>
> The same policy that prevails at our Penn street theatres will be observed at the Strand. Every courtesy will be extended to the patrons and every suggestion will be welcomed that will tend to benefit the amusement lovers of this part of the city.
>
> Our sincerest endeavor is to please our new friends in the northeastern section.
>
> *(Signed)*   CARR & SCHAD, Inc.
>
> *Become a Regular at the Strand*   *Complete Change of Program Daily*
>
> ### SCALE OF PRICES
> Adults, 13c; tax, 2c; total, 15c; Children 9c; tax, 1c; total, 10c

February 15, 1920, *Reading Eagle* ad announcing the opening of the Strand Theatre.

**The Strand Theatre at 9th and Spring Streets, circa 1931.
Photo courtesy of John Glase.**

reopened with the feature film, "Men of Boy's Town," starring Spencer Tracy and Mickey Rooney. The manager appointed by the new owner was Paul Esterly.

Over the years, the Strand was to have many managers, including Earl Hinkle, Clayton Evans, and Bluma Madeira, but those who loved this neighborhood picture palace with its distinctive huge box office rarely knew the name of the manager. However, they knew that the Strand was the place to go on a balmy summer evening to escape not only the heat but also the reality of life by buying a fifty-cent ticket to a thrilling double feature like "Rear Window" with Jimmy Stewart and Grace Kelly and "North By Northwest" starring Cary Grant. The Strand was where people went on a cold December evening, leaving early enough to sip a steaming cup of coffee at the Strand Restaurant to warm their bones before strolling over to the brightly-lit theatre to warm their hearts with the melodic crooning of Bing Crosby in "White Christmas." Reading High School cheerleaders cheered on the stage of the Strand at the school's athletic awards programs and employees of Wyomissing Industries sang Christmas carols in its auditorium at company holiday parties.

In 1956 this neighborhood film house changed hands again when the William Goldman chain purchased it, along with the Astor, from Schad. Unfortunately, television already had a stranglehold on the American public who seemed hypnotized by the little picture box which sat blinking in their living rooms. In an effort to woo back this fickle public, the Goldman chain booked Hollywood blockbusters like "Around the World in 80 Days" whose success can be seen by the seating reservation form which appeared in the January 19, 1958, edition of the *Eagle*. Note that January reservations were already filled. Goldman continued to draw the neighborhood crowds during the sixties by playing double features starring such favorites as Shirley MacLaine and Dean Martin, Gary Cooper, and Paul Newman. Thus, the Strand remained a viable part of the neighborhood until February 23, 1970, when tragedy in the form of fire struck down the old movie house. On that date, the *Reading Eagle* headline blared "Nine Companies Respond to Two Alarms," and, as the newspaper reported, the destruction was extensive, with the heaviest damage occurring in the balcony and rear portion of the theatre. The entrance lobby and theatre proper also sustained water and smoke damage. The fire, reported at 6:29 A.M. by a passerby, was believed to have started in the concession area, and by the time firemen arrived, thick, acrid smoke, whipped along by high winds, enveloped Spring Street. According to the account in

Reading Eagle ad for May 29, 1941, when Harry Schad took control of the Strand again.

14

Reading Eagle ad of December 25, 1954.

Reading Eagle ad of January 19, 1958.

the Reading newspaper, manager Bluma Madeira, visibly shaken by the conflagration, was led away in tears. Her brother, Clayton Evans, manager of the Astor, recounted that part of the movie house had been recently renovated. This renovation included a lobby roof, refurbished rest rooms, and repaired rear walls. The outtap to this first fire in the Strand's fifty-year history was sounded at 11:45 A.M. Three teenagers were later arrested for starting the blaze.

Another fire of suspicious origin hit the Strand on August 11, 1974, when juvenile investigators were called in to investigate three fires which occurred early that Sunday. The other arson targets were the Reading Y.M.C.A. and the company's Outer Station. The search centered on a teenager who was seen near the Strand at the time of the 7:01 A.M. blaze and was a suspect in all three fires which were ignited by a flammable liquid. This suspected arson damaged the stage and rear portion of the movie house which had been purchased by Fox Theater Management Corporation for $60,000 in January 1973 from Budco-Goldman Theaters, Inc. which had purchased the Strand from William Goldman Theaters, Inc. in 1972. This beloved neighborhood film landmark would never recover from these devastating fires.

In April 1975 the theatre was razed to make way for another of the ubiquitous golden arches of the McDonald's fast food chain. But those who loved this Ninth and Spring movie house knew that a treasured piece of their existence was gone, for the Strand, with its huge, brightly-lit marquee, its spacious auditorium, and its unique style, was one of a kind.

The Strand Theatre, circa 1948. Note the change in the marquee from the earlier photo. Photo courtesy of Elmer Quinn.

Damages Strand

Firemen Battle Theater Blaze

A fireman in the Reading Hose Co. snorkel gondola sprays water onto the roof of the Strand Theater from the 9th street side this morning and others climb ladders from apparatus on Spring street as a two-bell-alarm fire caused extensive damage to the concession and balcony areas of the 50-year-old-theater. Other photos on Page 17.—Eagle Photo.

Reading Eagle coverage of the first Strand fire - February 23, 1970.

(Opposite) August 11, 1974, *Eagle* coverage of the second fire to hit the Strand.

Police Seek Arsonist

City juvenile detectives continued their investigation today into three fires of suspicious origin early Sunday which damaged the vacant Strand Theater the former Reading Co. YMCA, and the Company's Outer Station.

A teenager suspect seen running near the Strand Theater, 9th and Spring Streets, at the time of the 7:01 a.m. blaze, is being sought in all three fires.

Fire officials said a flammable liquid was believed used to ignite the three structures.

The major damage at the former YMCA, 6th and Greenwich streets, was caused by smoke, according to Deputy Fire Chief Charles W. Schaeffer Jr.

A Reading Co. policeman saw smoke pouring from the northwest side of the second, third and fourth floors of the building at 4:38 a.m. when he made a routine check.

City police found that a door panel on the northeast corner of the building had been knocked out, apparently by the arsonist.

The fire, located on the second floor, burned door frames, and smoke filtered throughout the rest of the structure. Firemen remained at the scene an hour and a half.

The blaze at the theatre burned the stage area, the rear of the building and paint cans and solvents.

Deputy Fire Chief William H. Rehr III said he believes a flammable liquid was used.

At 7:35 a.m., while firemen were still battling the theater fire, a blaze was discovered at the Outer Station, 6th and Oley Streets.

Chief Rehr said an arsonist is suspected of climbing over the roof and into an old clock tower to gain entry to the boarded-up building.

Firemen had to break into the building to fight the blaze, which was confined to the southeast corner of the the building.

Accelerant Used

According to Deputy Chief Rehr, a flammable liquid was poured on a partition and two doorways nearby in the southeast corner of the first floor.

Two holes were believed to have been gouged into a wall by the arsonist, apparently to aid the burning of the fire.

Firemen left the Strand Theater at 9:26 a.m., and they remained at the Outer Station until 8:30 a.m.

Although the three buildings are vacant, the former YMCA is in the process of being sold and the Strand Theatre was sold over a year ago.

Hope Rescue Mission is negotiating a final purchase settlement with the Reading Co. for the former YMCA.

The Rev. George T. Davis Jr., mission superintendent, said he is not sure how the fire will affect the sale negotiations, although a down payment has already been made.

The theater was purchased in January, 1973 by Fox Theaters Management Corp. for $60,000. It was bought from Budco-Goldman Theaters Inc., which had purchased the old theater from William Goldman Theaters Inc., in 1972.

The former Outer Station was rejected in June as a site of a Berks Area Reading Transportation Authority (BARTA) garage.

In other city fire calls, a burning mop was extinguished at 11:32 a.m. at 702 Penn St. Spontaneous combustion was cited as the cause.

Firemen responded to false alarms at 12:05 a.m. at 7th and Penn Streets, and at 11:54 p.m. at McClellan and Scott Streets.

Smoke Billows From Burning Theater

A ladder truck waits at the rear of the Strand Theater, 9th and Spring Streets, early Sunday, as firemen fight a fire which damaged the stage area, paints and solvents in the rear of the vacant structure. The fire at the theater was one of three within three hours believed to have been started by an arsonist.

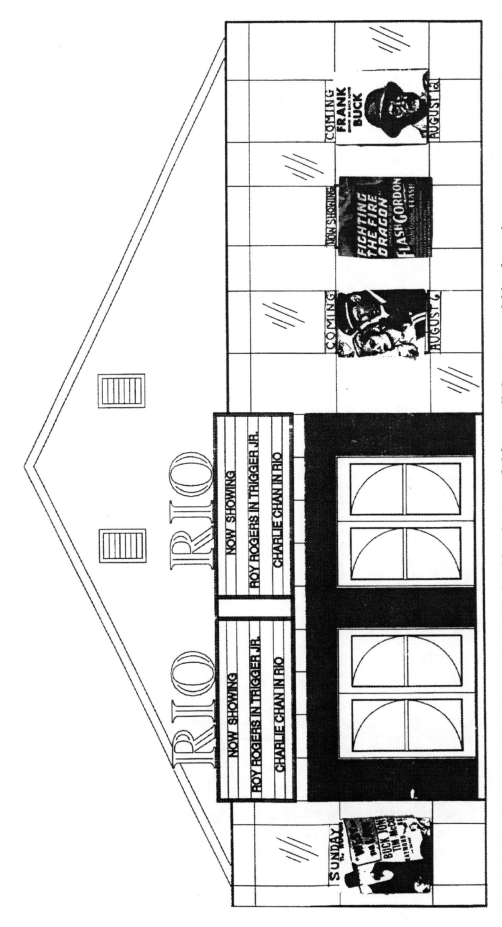

A computer drawing of the Rio by John Wade. No photos of this small theatre could be found.

5. The Rio

Another neighborhood survivor was the little picture house in the 600 block of Schuylkill Avenue where, on Thanksgiving Day, 1911, Ben Zerr opened Reading's first neighborhood theatre, the Olivet. In 1913, this building at 647 Schuylkill Avenue changed marquees to become the Schuylkill Avenue Picture House. According to Paul Glase's *Annals*, one of Mr. Zerr's early ventures was the opening of an "air dome," or open air auditorium, next to the theatre. Zerr also featured the showing of "Quo Vadis" with reserved seats at twenty-five and fifty cents, with a box office at George Hintz's book store. Assisting in the building of this northwest Reading film enterprise was Theodore "Ted" Nyquist, Sr., who then became its first operator (Nyquist also operated an "air dome" on the lot later occupied by Vanity Fair Silk Mills). However, in 1928 the theatre closed and the building became a market house, and, later, a tabernacle.

Ben Zerr's Schuylkill Avenue Theatre at 647 Schuylkill Avenue. In 1936, it became the Rio. Photo courtesy of John Glase.

Fortunately, to the advantage of the neighborhood, and Reading in general, the theatre was reopened on April 11, 1936, by Henry Sork and Harry Block who refurbished the interior, constructed a new marquee and entranceway, and rechristened it the Rio. Eventually, Mr. Sork took over as the sole operator, appointing Pauline Gilberry and John Leiss as managers.

This small movie house showed a variety of films over the years, including first-runs, but it is best remembered for its westerns and serials by the kids who flocked to its ticket window during the forties to see Roy Rogers, Gene Autry, Sunset Carson, and other sagebrush heroes kick up the dust as they chased villain Roy Barcroft across the silver screen. The Rio had no candy counter. Instead,

**THE NEW
RIO THEATRE**
647 Schuylkill Ave.
OPENING SAT., APRIL 11
AT 11:00 A. M.

LUPE   IAN
VELEZ HUNTER
IN
"The Morals of Marcus"
FIRST SHOWING IN READING

ADDED: FOR THE KIDDIES
First Chapter "Rex and Rint"
"POPEYE"   "BETTY BOOP"

ADMISSION
Children, 10c. Adults, Mat., 15c; Eve., 25c
Continuous Sat. and Sun. Showing Only the Best Product of the Major Producers

**Opening ad for the Rio Theatre.
Reading Eagle - April 11, 1936.**

Rio film ad with dinnerware offer for "The Ladies."

Combined ad for Max Korr's Plaza and Rio Theatres.

Firemen climb ladders while others fight the blaze on ground level as fire broke out in the Joseph Zerbe Hardware Store, 649-51 Schuylkill Ave., about 12:30 p.m. today. Heavy smoke pours from the building, the former Rio Theater.—Eagle Photos.

Reading Eagle coverage of the May 2, 1962, Zerbe Hardware store fire which destroyed the former Rio Theatre building at 647 Schuylkill Avenue.

huge metal machines displaying chew-challenging treats like Black Crows and Jujubes stood just inside the lobby awaiting wartime nickels as motivation to drop their boxes of precious cargo. In addition, the Rio patron could choose to sit in a standard seat or, if so inclined, settle into a double-size throne at the end of the aisle as film dreams clicked out of the projector mounted in the upstairs projection booth, its single beam of light illuminating the tiny particles of dust which floated over the heads of spellbound moviegoers.

Like many other theatres of its time, the Rio also ran special kiddie programs at which youngsters could win various prizes. For example, the April 11, 1941, *Reading Eagle* ad for the Rio carried the following announcement in order to entice young patrons to part with their movie money.

BOYS' AND GIRLS'
BIG EASTER PARTY
AT OUR SATURDAY MATINEE
FREE-30-CHICKS-30
6-RABBITS-6

Fran Gabrielli of Mount Penn recalls a pet contest at this Schuylkill Avenue movie house in which her sister entered a white chicken wearing a red ribbon around its neck. The judging was very close but the small, well-dressed fowl came in ahead of a rabbit for first prize. Of course, these special promotions were not always popular with mothers who were left with crying children or needy pets. However, the management of the Rio did attempt to make up for the inconveniences they had caused these mothers by presenting "Dinnerware Nights" when mom might pick up a soup dish or a dinner plate for the mere price of a twenty-five cent ticket.

By 1948, Max Korr Enterprises was operating the Rio and attempting to revive its popularity by bringing in first-run features, but it was too late. Over the years of its existence, the little theatre had served the neighborhood well, but with the demise of the Hollywood studio system and the advent of television, the old picture house began to falter. Its final film ad appeared in the March 3, 1951, edition of the *Reading Eagle* which announced that, after that date, the theater would be temporarily closed. In addition, the ad advised dish collectors to "Get Your Dishes On Sunday" at Korr's Plaza Theatre in Reading.

Sadly, this was not a temporary closing. Thus, the film playing at the time, "King Solomon's Mines," became the last film ever to play the Rio. In July of 1951, Zerbe and Company contractors bought the building and opened the Zerbe Hardware store which remained in business until May 2, 1962, when a general alarm fire, punctuated by two explosions, demolished what had been Ben Zerr's "little picture house." The site is presently a vacant lot.

The last film ad for the Rio Theatre announcing its "Temporary Closing" as it appeared in the March 3, 1951, edition of the *Reading Eagle*.

6. The Shillington

The same year that the "talkies" emerged upon moviedom's scene, the Roxie came to Shillington, for on November 17, 1929, Stanley Warkoczski opened this neighborhood's first movie theatre at 22 New Holland Avenue. Since no advertising can be found in the theatre sections of the newspapers of the day, it must be assumed that Mr. Warkoczski was operating on a tight budget. However, the Roxy survived until 1935 when Mr. Joseph Shverha bought the film house and changed its name to the Shillington Theatre, a name which would remain until its closing in 1986. Mr. Shverha ran the theatre on New Holland Avenue until 1949 when he decided to move to a busier location at 29 East Lancaster Avenue in the borough. It was at that time that the building on New Holland Avenue was taken over by the Shillington Athletic Association.

The "new" Shillington opened to much fanfare as crowds lined the sidewalk on Saturday, September 3, 1949, to see their newest neighborhood entertainment center. At approximately 6 P.M., the doors swung open and people hurried in to grab a velvet-lined seat to see Esther Williams come splashing onto the brand-new screen in her latest water pic, "Neptune's Daughter." Mr. Shverha and his wife (who often sat in the ticket booth) would bring the best in movie entertainment to the people of Shillington for approximately the next twenty years. The theatre was closed on Sundays but the remaining six days of the week, this little neighborhood movie house offered top-notch entertainment in a sparkling clean building, for the Shverhas ran a very tidy house, refusing to open a snack bar or allow patrons to bring food into their theatre. However, Ira Bergman of Shillington recalls that Mr. Shverha would advertise free Hershey bars at the matinees in an effort to entice the younger patrons to attend these shows so that they would not bother the adults at the evening performances.

The *Reading Eagle* ad of September 2, 1949, which announced the opening of the "new" Shillington Theatre at 29 East Lancaster Avenue.

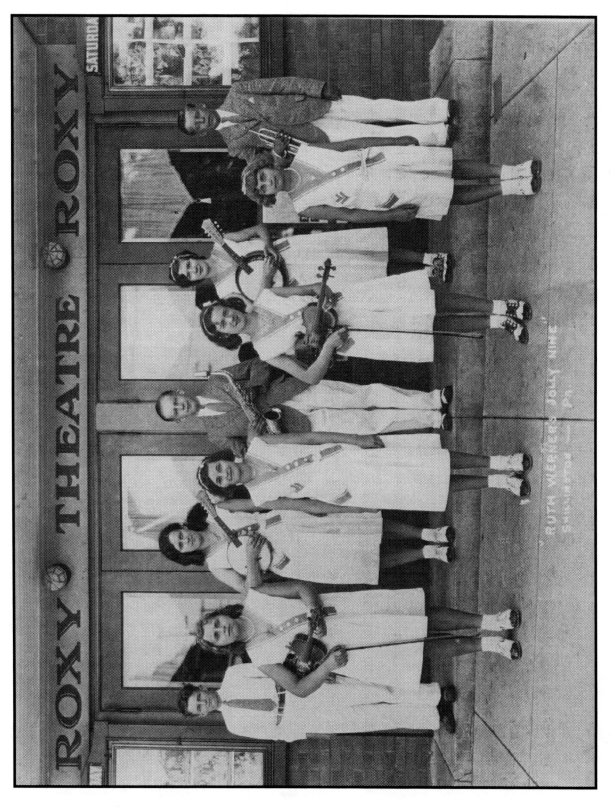

"Ruth Werner's Jolly Nine" poses in front of the Roxy Theatre at 22 New Holland Avenue in Shillington, circa 1930's. In 1935, this became the Shillington Theatre when Joseph Shverha bought the business. It later moved to Lancaster Avenue. Photo courtesy of Ira Bergman of Shillington.

The September 3, 1949, opening night of the "new" Shillington Theatre at 29 E. Lancaster Avenue.
Photo courtesy of Ira Bergman.

The opening night crowd at the "new" Shillington Theatre.
Photo courtesy of Ira Bergman.

Another memory of this neighborhood theatre comes from Donald Mellinger of Wernersville who worked as an usher from 1938 to 1941, before the theatre moved to Lancaster Avenue. He remembers carrying huge, heavy boxes of dishes from the basement to hand out to the ladies who stocked their china closets with these future treasures. Another former employee, Shirley Christman of Mt. Penn, who worked the ticket booth during her high school years, remembers Mr. Shverha as a no-nonsense theatre operator who patrolled the aisles on a regular basis. Anyone bold enough to put his feet up on the seat in front would feel a sharp blow on the back of his chair.

In 1968, the Shverhas sold their little movie house to Marshal and Roed, Inc., who hired Marguerite Nagle as manager. The theatre continued to operate as a single screen entity until May 21, 1978, when the movie page of the *Reading Eagle* announced the arrival of the "Twin Stars," declaring that the Shillington would now be known as the "Shillington Stars." As the newest twin-screen film house in Berks County, the theatre reopened on Wednesday, May 24, 1978, with the hit film, "Saturday Night Fever," playing in Star 1 and the sci-fi thriller, "Close Encounters of the Third Kind," featured in Star 2.

However, those who frequented the little movie house could hardly imagine the building so divided without causing major claustrophobia among its patrons. Unfortunately, even though it was the only game in town, attendance declined drastically over the years. For example, on Christmas Eve of 1954, an SRO crowd applauded the closing scene of the holiday treat, "White Christmas," as snow filled the screen while the film's stars crooned the title tune. Conversely, on Christmas Day of 1983, five people sat silently as snow fell behind the closing credits for the wonderful holiday release, "A Christmas Story."

By 1986, the film house was being run by the Fox Theatre Management, with Lori George as manager. It was in that year that the final show occurred, with the last movie ad appearing on September 1 for the films, "A Fine Mess" and "Club Paradise." Ironically, this small brick building where people came to worship movie stars became a place where people came to worship God as the Grace Fellowship Church bought the structure in 1987. As of this writing, church services are still being held within its converted interior. To its credit, the congregation opted not to tear down this piece of Shillington history.

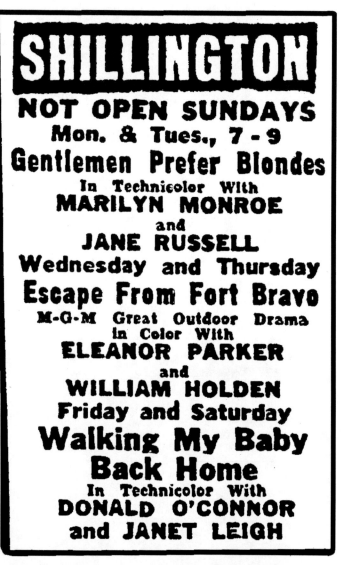

Reading Eagle ad of February 21, 1954, when Joseph Shverha owned the Shillington Theatre, and it did not open on Sundays.

The Shillington Theatre reopens as the "Twin Stars" as these *Reading Eagle* ads from May 21 and May 24, 1978, illustrate.

28

7. THE LAUREL

This 300 seat neighborhood theatre was opened by William Heckman on September 5, 1934, on the site of the former Rosedale Chapel at 1107 Elizabeth Avenue in Laureldale. Its opening ad in the *Reading Eagle* that day boasted of a "New Western Electric Sound System - New Silver Sound Screen, Carpets, and Draperies." Those lucky enough to attend the opening settled comfortably into cushioned seats with wooden backs to watch in glee while child star Shirley Temple cavorted on the screen in the film, "Baby Take A Bow." Also advertised in that same edition of the local newspaper was a special Saturday matinee which was coming up for the kiddies. Paul Glase recounts that Martin Roberts took over the movie house next, appointing Samuel Felt as manager. Then, Harry Friedland bought the property and became the new manager of the Laurel.

Friedland ran the theatre through the forties and into the fifties, showing such upbeat fare of the day as "Scudda Hoo, Scudda Hay," with June Haver, while claiming that the "healthfully air-conditioned theatre" (actually air-cooled) was a "Short Drive for Good Entertainment." However, the Laurel closed its doors in 1953 for a short time before William Richter, presently of Mount Penn, bought the business and reopened the neighborhood film house.

Richter had started his career at the Majestic Theatre in Mount Penn where he had been assistant manager before going off to help fight World War II. After the war, he returned to the Majestic where he continued his training in theatre management under the GI Bill. Thus, he was well-equipped to take on the responsibilities which came with theatre management. During Richter's tenure, a screen was purchased from the Loew's Colonial Theatre in Reading and installed within the small confines of the Laurel, making it possible to show CinemaScope films. Because the screen from the larger theatre stretched almost from wall to wall, patrons in the small space of the auditorium felt as though they were really "in the movies." Richter also obtained some 3-D films for showing in his movie house. However, he chose to show them without 3-D technology, thus eliminating the need for the clumsy, cardboard, spaceman glasses. The Laurel also had a television room with a projection TV for patrons who preferred the few programs then being broadcast by the fledgling industry to the action being shown on the screen.

Bill Richter's operation lasted until 1955 when the mortgage on the building was foreclosed. Since he owned the business but not the building, Bill had to close his theatre. That same year, however, a neighbor bought the building and agreed to buy all of the theatre's equipment from Richter in

Reading Eagle ad which heralded the opening of the Laurel Theatre on September 5, 1934.

29

The Laurel Theatre on Elizabeth Avenue in Laureldale, circa 1946. Photo courtesy of Elmer Quinn.

Another view of the Laurel.
Photo courtesy of Elmer Quinn.

return for the right to continue using the original name on the marquee. Thus, another attempt to resurrect the Laurel was made by Ed Foley who had managed a few other local theatres and now took over the lease for the Laureldale operation. The new manager hoped to boost sagging attendance by featuring special programs. For example, Tuesdays and Wednesdays were "Encore Nights" at which time hit films of recent years were shown. In order to gauge moviegoers' preferences, Foley invited patrons to send in their requests for movies they wished to see. Another promotional draw was the "Gigantic Horror Show" at which the management awarded a "Sweetheart Pass" to "anyone having the courage to remain in the theatre for the entire show." But the promotions were not enough to keep the crowds coming, and that same year as its reopening, the Laurel closed its doors and silenced its projectors for the last time.

The original building which housed the Laurel Theatre still stands at 1107 Elizabeth Avenue in Laureldale, although it has been extensively renovated since a 1990 fire. Over the years since the closing of the motion picture house, a variety of firms have conducted business at this address, including a beer distributor, a plumbing firm, and a basement waterproofing company. But to those who remember it best, its patrons and neighbors, it will always be the home of the "little Laurel."

January 1, 1956, *Reading Eagle* ad for "Encore Nights" at the Laurel Theatre.

The Penn Theatre on the northwest corner of Sixth and Penn Avenues in West Reading, circa 1939. This theatre was built at a cost of $100,000 and featured a "bowl" floor.
Photo courtesy of George M. Meiser, IX.   Photo by Earl R. Anderson.

8. THE PENN

In the summer of 1939, Wilmer and Vincent purchased the Ruth estate at Sixth and Penn Avenues in West Reading for the purpose of building a theatre on the site. According to an article which ran in the *Reading Eagle* on December 23, 1939, this movie house in the western suburbs of Berks County was to be opened at a cost of $100,000 and was to feature a "bowl floor," a new idea in theatre construction. This gave the front section of seats a slight rise, thus relieving patrons of eye strain from looking up at the screen. Another innovation for the comfort of theatregoers were seats which rose with the patron. As George M. Meiser, IX, notes in Volume One of *The Passing Scene*, the Penn was the last of the large neighborhood movie houses to be built.

On Christmas Day, 1939, the theatre opened with the showing of the gangster saga, "The Roaring Twenties," starring James Cagney and Humphrey Bogart. Readers of that day's edition of the *Reading Eagle* were apprised of the fact that, at this picture house, "parking space is always available," a statement that already portended one of the reasons for the demise of the downtown theatres. Moreover, the Wilmer and the Vincent ad campaign boasted that, with the opening

> ...we bring to the heart of your community one of the finest suburban theatres in the
> entire State. Handsomely decorated and furnished; comfortably seated; ventilated
> and equipped with the latest improvements in projection and sound engineering.
> We want you to feel that this is your theatre, built for your amusement...

Among the managers of this West Reading picture house were Thomas A. McCarthy (1940 - 1943), Howard Whittle (1943 - 1950's), and John Ivanitch (1954). Both the popularity of the theatre and manager Whittle were heralded in an article which appeared in the August 4, 1943, edition of *The Moviegoer*, Wilmer and Vincent's theatre publication which was given to patrons of their film establishments. The article, entitled "Manager Whittle Popular with West Reading Theatregoers," told how Whittle had gained a "wide circle of friends" stretching throughout the surrounding communities, including Wyomissing, Wyomissing Hills, Berkshire Heights, and other nearby neighborhoods whose residents "are finding complete enjoyment at the comfortable and cool Penn Theatre." In addition, the writer states that "the popularity of the theatre continues to increase, and once inside the auditorium, the hot sultry weather outside is soon forgotten."

The price of a ticket at the time for all these amenities was a mere twenty-eight cents. Kids under twelve were even luckier, for eleven cents was all they needed to gain entrance to this neighborhood palace, a great bargain since most shows consisted of a double feature and, as the ads boasted, "Extra Added Good Shorts." There were, however, a few rare times when ticket buyers did not get their money's worth. In an article which appeared in the August 26, 1961, edition of the *Reading Eagle Sunday Magazine*, Wallace Hill, a projectionist at the Penn, recalls a most embarrassing dilemma which occurred one evening in 1940 when he discovered that reel one of a film he was scheduled to show that evening was missing. Moreover, he had two copies of reel seven. How could he show the film? Hill searched frantically for reel one while the audience began clapping for the delayed show to begin. But reel one was nowhere to be found. By now, the manager of the Penn had been informed of the bad news. With a great deal of courage, he explained the dilemma to the patrons and told them that the first twenty minutes of the film would not be shown. The mystery was solved, however, when a theatre in the coal regions found that they had two number one reels of the film and no number sevens. Reels

IT'S BING'S BEST!

Bing CROSBY
Dorothy LAMOUR

in

DIXIE

with

Marjorie Reynolds
Billy de Wolfe

In TECHNICOLOR

Now Playing At the Embassy Theatre

LOSES HEROINES

Franchot Tone has hard luck with his heroines. In "True to Life" he lost Mary Martin to Dick Powell. In "Five Graves to Cairo," Anne Baxter dies, and in "The Hour Before the Dawn," Tone learns his wife, Veronica Lake, is a Nazi agent and he kills her.

Penn Theatre ad in Wilmer and Vincent's August 4, 1943, *Moviegoer.*

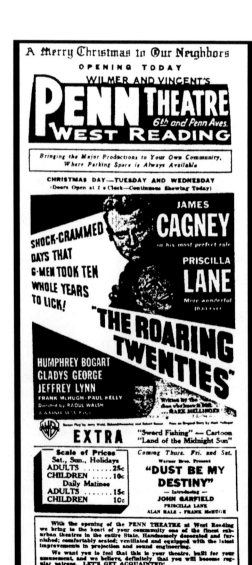

Reading Eagle ad for the opening of the Penn Theatre on Christmas Day, 1939.

were exchanged, and the next evening, patrons saw the entire film.

The Penn continued to show quality films to the inhabitants of Western Berks until June 1, 1954, when what appears to be the last motion picture shown at this theatre, "Sabre Jet," was featured. The site was then leased to Orth Music House, and later, Reifsnyder Music. The Olympian Ballroom, operated by Jerry and Linda Theodossiou Topaz, now occupies the main auditorium, while the William H. Diller Jewelry store does business on the northeast corner.

Ironically, according to Eugene Deeter who operated the Majestic Theatre in Mount Penn, this theatre on Penn Avenue was to be christened the Majestic and the Majestic, which also opened in 1939, was to be the Penn. However, due to a mixup in delivery of the marquees, the names were reversed. But regardless of the name on its marquee, this "moving picture house" at 601-603 Penn Avenue always delivered top entertainment.

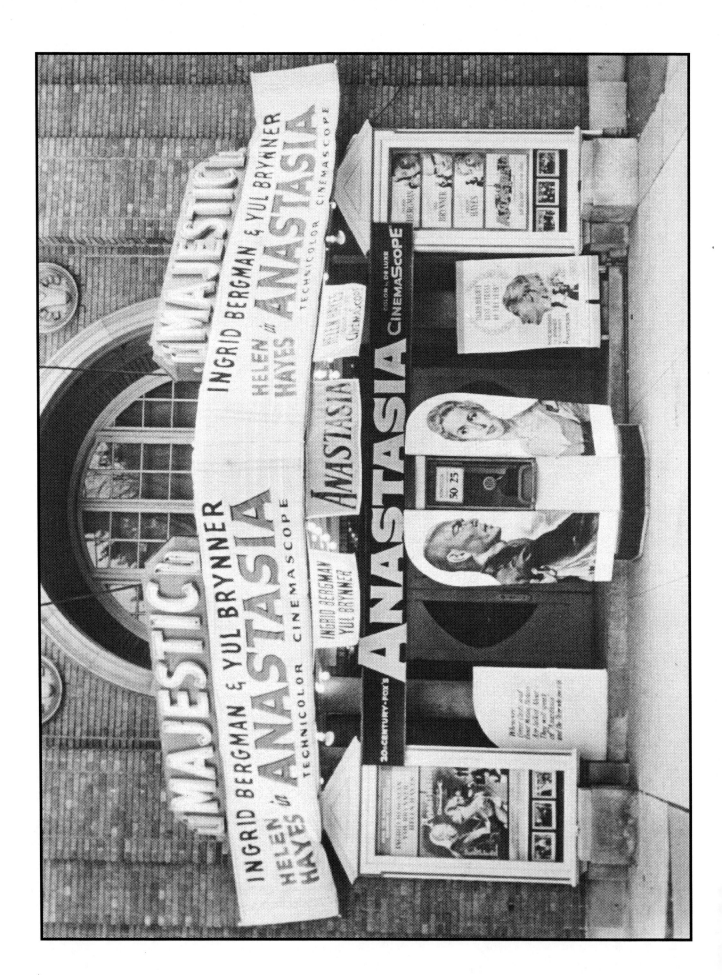

9. THE MAJESTIC

The opening of the Majestic Theatre in Mount Penn. *Reading Eagle* - November 10, 1939.

On November 10, 1939, Eugene Deeter bought a ticket to the show in the newly-opened Wilmer and Vincent theatre at 23rd and Filbert Streets in Mount Penn. That theatre was the Majestic. Sixteen years later, Mr. Deeter would take over its management.

According to the writings of Paul E. Glase, the building which housed the Majestic was built in the early part of the century and had previously been used as a gymnasium and auditorium before being converted to a

Reading Eagle ad - January 6, 1949.

(Opposite) The Majestic Theatre at 23rd and Filbert Streets in Mount Penn, circa 1956. Photo by Harrison Deeter. Courtesy of Mr. and Mrs. Eugene Deeter.

theatre by Wilmer and Vincent. The feature film chosen for the grand premiere was Darryl F. Zanuck's production of "The Rains Came," starring Tyrone Power and Myrna Loy. The doors opened that evening at 6:15, with admission prices of twenty-five cents for adults and ten cents for children. For this "astronomical" sum, patrons were treated to the feature film, a cartoon, a short subject, and the Fox news. On Saturday, there was a continuous showing of the program so that if a patron arrived late, he or she could simply stay for the next show. By May of 1940, Zimmerman and Friedland had assumed control of the Majestic, where Harry Friedland would remain until the fifties with William Richter as assistant manager.

During the forties and fifties, the Majestic continued to run the typical neighborhood theatre fare, including the popular "kiddie shows" and "special enticement" programs like the one which was advertised in the January 6, 1949, edition of the *Reading Eagle*. Patrons attending that show would not only see the feature film, "I Am a Fugitive from a Chain Gang," but also receive a free record and a chance to win a record player. Another exciting program was the one which was advertised in the January 20, 1950, edition of the *Eagle*. This one featured the popular comedy team of Bud Abbott and Lou Costello in the film, "Abbott and Costello Meet the Killer," along with Chapter 4 of "King of the Rocketmen," three color cartoons, candy on the house, and "Free to Some Lucky Girl or Boy a Schwinn Bicycle." It was every kid's dream show! Also appearing in the Majestic's ad for that day was a call for drivers, male or female, who would be admitted free to the theatre if they would bring three or more patrons to the show.

Then in the mid-fifties, the man whom most patrons remember as "Mr. Majestic" leased the

Reading Eagle ad for January 20, 1950, Kiddies' show and call for drivers.

(Opposite) The Majestic in Mount Penn, circa 1956. According to former operator, Eugene Deeter, the promotional materials for both "War and Peace" and "Anastasia" were obtained from the Embassy Theatre in Reading.
Photo by Harrison Deeter. Courtesy of Mr. and Mrs. Eugene Deeter.

neighborhood movie house from the Mount Penn Fire Company. He was to be its last manager. Under Eugene Deeter's operation, this house of film was quite successful, a success which might be attributed to his willingness to feature the avant-garde films which were becoming a staple of Hollywood in the fifties and sixties. According to Tony Lucia, a *Reading Eagle* staff writer who wrote the article, "A Movie House Crumbles," for the February 19, 1984, edition of the local paper, Mr. Deeter received considerable flak from church organizations for showing these films. However, as Lucia points out, many of these films are highly regarded today. The Majestic also drew thousands of patrons for its showings of wilderness films during this time period.

People remember various things about this movie house that were unique, like the brightly-patterned curtains that hung from its stage or the rumors of a ghost that haunted its auditorium. According to a story which appears in Charles J. Adams III's *Ghost Stories of Berks County Book Two*, the Majestic is said to be haunted by a ghost whose noises and footsteps have been heard by several employees. Adams relates that one former employee, Ruth Sell, claims to have seen a white shadow and heard muffled voices.

Unfortunately, the ghosts of the Majestic are all that remain today, for in February of 1984, this neighborhood film house was forced to close its doors due to rising fuel costs and increasing competition from the large theatre chains which now proliferate America's suburbs. The last film to play the Majestic was, ironically, the Mel Brooks production, "To Be or Not To Be." Alas, it was not to be. After the theatre closed, the building was rented out for various functions, with a renovation being completed in 1994 by the owners, the Mount Penn Fire Company. But the old theatre still echoes to the laughter of kids for it now houses the Antietam Academy Daycare Center. But nobody gives away free candy bars.

Eugene Deeter was well-known in local theatre circles, having managed various film houses before taking over the operation of the Majestic. Through these associations, he met many of the stars who came to Reading on promotional tours, even becoming friends with some. One of these friendships was with Bob Nolan and the Sons of the Pioneers who always made it a point to get together with Deeter whenever they were in the area. Eugene treasures the autographed photo which was given to him by this famous Western musical group which co-starred in so many films. Deeter has many interesting stories to tell relative to other stars who appeared in the area in the past. One such story concerns an appearance at the Astor in downtown Reading by Boris Karloff, Van Heflin, Richard Long, and Julie London who were here to promote the film, "Taproots."

It seems that Eugene and a friend had learned that the actors would be leaving from the Reading Airport after their

The Majestic Theatre in Mount Penn, circa 1956.
Photo by Harrison Deeter.
Courtesy of Mr. and Mrs. Eugene Deeter.

appearance, so the two movie buffs decided to try to meet the celebrities there. As Deeter and his friend were about to race out to Bern Township, they were stopped by a young boy who had overheard their conversation and was now pleading with them to take him along to meet "the Frankenstein Monster." They agreed to let him tag along. When they arrived at their destination, the starstruck trio spotted the celebrities sitting in the airport's restaurant having a quick bite to eat before taking off for filmland. Deeter recalls that the three fans hurried into the eating establishment to ask for autographs. Moreover, he remembers that the Hollywood stars were most gracious about signing their names, especially Karloff and Heflin. However, two events occurred which will stick in Deeter's mind forever. First, he and his friend

were so excited about meeting the stars that they forgot about the youngster they had reluctantly brought with them. Now they couldn't find him! By calling his name and searching diligently, they finally located him hiding under a table where he had scrambled to escape "the monster." When no amount of coaxing would bring him out, Deeter and his friend nervously explained the situation to Karloff who laughed uproariously and then gently coaxed the boy from his hiding place. An even funnier (and more embarrassing) incident took place when Eugene's friend bent over to obtain Julie London's autograph, and his jacket cuff plopped on the piece of pie the star was eating. Ever the gracious lady, Miss London kept right on eating the damaged dessert.

One of the 50's MGM hits which played the Majestic Theatre. *Reading Eagle* - April 28, 1957.

42

10. DOWNTOWN THEATRES

THE RAJAH

In July of 1870, workers began to erect a building at 135 North Sixth Street which was to contain a market house and Masonic Temple. However, Paul Glase relates that the panic of 1873 - 74 prevented completion so the property was sold by the sheriff to George D. Stitzel, William Nolan, and William Shomo. Using plans made by Philip Bissinger, the new owners erected a two-story brick building on the site. They then leased the second floor to the Harmonie Maennerchor which held balls, bazaars, masquerades, and concerts; thus, the property became known as Maennerchor Hall. When the Maennerchor moved to new quarters on North Sixth Street, the building was leased by the Reading Turn Verein.

Glase's writings reveal that James Nolan and John Mishler purchased an interest in the structure in 1896, organizing the Academy Company. It was then that the necessary changes were made and the former market house became the Academy of Music, with the Reading Turn Verein continuing to occupy the top floors. The renovated structure was 80 feet in width and 230 feet in depth, with a grand entrance 14 feet wide by 100 feet deep. On the south side was the Acad-

The Rajah Theatre in 1996. It is the last of the old theatres in Reading still being used as an entertainment center.
Photo courtesy of Dixie Kreider of Kenhorst.

(Opposite) The Rajah Theatre on North Sixth Street in Reading sometime in the 1940's when Tony Pastor came to town.
Photo courtesy of Elmer Quinn.

emy Cafe and on the north side was the office of the Union Transfer. The Academy, which was the first theatre in Reading built on the ground floor, was divided into three sections: the gallery with 306 seats; the balcony with 473; and the parlor chairs, orchestra, and orchestra circle section with seating for 892 patrons. Various size medallions dominated the ceiling and dome from which was suspended a massive prism chandelier. The beautiful frescoes, displaying foliage of flowers and sprays and rare tropical birds in rich plumage, were based on original designs by Philadelphia's Louis MacLaurin. In its years as the Academy of Music, the 1,671 seat theatre presented approximately 4,044 dramatic and musical shows featuring appearances by stars like Lillian Russel, Tyrone Power, Eddie Foy, Ethel and Lionel Barrymore, and Douglass Fairbanks.

In 1917, the building changed hands again when it was purchased by the Rajah Temple and renamed the Rajah Theatre. Under the direction of the trustees of the Shrine, George F. Eisenbrown, Potentate, and J. Edward Wanner and J. Wilmer Fisher, Directors, Phil Levy was installed as resident manager with William Cook as stage manager. The theatre opened in the fall of 1917 with a spectacular street parade featuring camels, Arabs, and a long list of Shriners. The opening attraction on stage was "The Garden of Allah," featuring Sarah Truex and Howard Gould. Various luminaries appeared on the stage of the Rajah during the next four years. These included Al Jolson, Otis Skinner, the Dolly Sisters, and Alfred Lunt. Tragically, fire struck the Rajah on May 10, 1921, destroying the front of the building and causing damage of more than $100,000. The entire interior was ruined by fire and smoke. Undaunted, the Rajah Temple members rebuilt the building immediately.

After the new building was completed, the theatre was leased to Wilmer and Vincent who went on to operate it for ten years, during which time they

Dish night at the Rajah. *Reading Eagle* - January 14, 1943.

45

presented a mixture of vaudeville, stage attractions, and a few important motion pictures such as D. W.

Griffith's "Way Down East." Appearing on stage during the Wilmer and Vincent reign were Fay Bainter, Ethel Barrymore, Basil Rathbone, Fanny Brice, and other stars of the day. Also, in 1923, the Orpheum stock company was transferred to the Rajah and, under the direction of William Naughton and Rose Ludwig, became the Rajah Players. Managers during these years included George W. Carr, Frank D. Hill, and Frank O'Brien. Frank Harms and George Gross were among the orchestra leaders. The Wilmer and Vincent organization attempted a variety of innovative programs, including "the Supper Show" which was held every Saturday evening at 6' oclock "for those who want to avoid the afternoon and evening crowds," as stated in an ad which ran in the October 11, 1925, edition of the *Reading Eagle*. Another feature was the regular children's matinee from 1:30 to 3:30 PM with a special admission rate.

Wilmer and Vincent relinquished operation of the Rajah in May of 1931, with the Board of Governors of the Shrine in charge again during the 1932 - 1933 season and William Heckman as manager. Irwin Yates managed for a brief time in 1933 before Finch and Ahl took over for a three year run of motion picture double feature programs. The year 1937 saw the Rajah Theatre Company in charge, with Jay Emanuel and C. G. Keeney as executives. Calvin Lieberman was the house manager. During this period, stage attractions, concerts, and motion pictures were featured. Also part of the program were free dish nights for all ladies who purchased a 25¢ ticket. In 1946, the lease passed to Keeney who continued

Reading Eagle ad of January 31, 1954, announcing the upcoming visit of Gene Autry to the Rajah.

RAJAH

FRIDAY & SATURDAY

King of the Vibra Harp
Master of the Drums

Lionel

Hampton

AND
HIS ORCHESTRA

Featuring

**Winni   Brown
Roland   Burton
Herman McCoy**

RED & CURLY
"DRUM BOOGIE"

MARA KIM
"CHINA'S BOOGIE"

ON THE SCREEN
CHARLIE CHAN AND HIS
MOST BAFFLING CASE

The **Chinese Ring**

ROBERT   MANTAN
WINTERS • MORELAND

Due to Shrine Activities There Will
Be No Show This Thursday

RAJAH   THURSDAY
                    FRIDAY
                    SATURDAY

NOTICE
Continuous Show Daily
STAGE SHOW
Thursday, Friday
at 3:15—7:05—9:30

Your Alltime Singing Favorite
Of the Famous
GLENN MILLER ORCH.

Ray

Eberle

And His Popular
ORCHESTRA
Featuring
ROSEMARY CALVIN
"LOVELY LADY OF SONG"

BILLY MAXTED
NOTED ARRANGER

Extra! Added Attraction!
DIRECT FROM HOLLYWOOD

**Robert
Alda**

Warner Bros. Screen Star!
Starred in the
Following Pictures—
"RHAPSODY IN BLUE"
"CLOAK AND DAGGER"
"THE MAN I LOVE"
AND MANY OTHERS

ANN RUSSEL
"LUSCIOUS LADY—WITH
LAUGHING LYRICS"

MAGE & KARR
America's Newest
Dancing Stars

Novelty Community Sing
Featuring at the Organ
**"Les"
Hoffmaster**

ON THE SCREEN—
DAGWOOD AND BLONDIE
IN PLENTY OF FUN FOR ALL
Blondie in the Dough
PENNY   ★   ARTHUR
SINGLETON   LAKE

Special Announcement
Regarding The
Appearances Of

**FRED
WARING**
and the
Pennsylvanians

Wednesday, April 14
7 and 9:30 P. M.

RAJAH THEATRE

ALL SEATS ARE SOLD FOR
BOTH PERFORMANCES.
NAMES WILL BE ACCEPTED
FOR A WAITING LIST, FOR
ACCOMMODATION IN THE
EVENT OF CANCELLATIONS
150 STANDING ROOM TICK-
ETS FOR EACH PERFORM-
ANCE, NOW ON SALE AT
HANGEN'S MUSIC HOUSE,
47 SOUTH 6TH ST., PRICED
AT $1.50 PLUS FEDERAL
AND CITY TAXES.

COMING IN PERSON

JOSE ITURBI
In a Duo-Piano Recital With
AMPARO ITURBI
RAJAH

One Performance Only 8:30 P. M.
Tues. Evening, April 20

Prices: $1.95, $2.60, $3.25, $3.90. This
includes tax. Mail orders now. (Enclose
Self-Addressed Stamped Envelope). Sale
begins March 15. Hangen's Music House,
43 South 6th St.   Phone 4-1281.

Rajah   TODAY-FRI.-SAT.

Continuous Show
Doors Open 12:45 P. M.

Yes! We Play All the Big Bands!

RAY McKINLEY
His Vocals—His Drums
America's Most Versatile
ORCHESTRA
featuring
JENNIE FRILEY

PEEWEE HUNT
And His Band
ORIGINATOR OF
'12th Street Rag'
On Capitol Records

Reading Eagle ads showing a sampling of the many acts which appeared on the Rajah stage in 1948. Also opposite page.

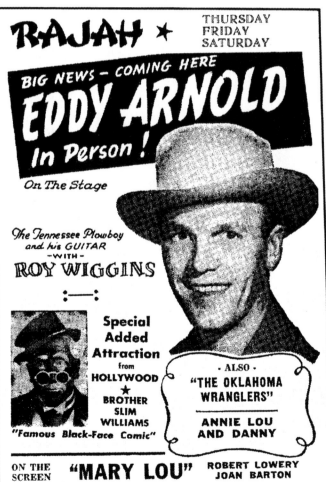

Cowboy Here to Stay, Autry Tells Small Fry

Capacity Crowds See Film Star On Rajah Stage

By DICK PETERS
Times Staff Writer

THIS may come as quite a shock to some of the small fry, but the space cadet or rocket ranger never will replace the American cowboy.

From a slightly partisan viewpoint, that is the belief of Gene Autry.

And Autry is one cowpoke who has thrown a saddle on enough greenbacks that he needn't care whether the nation's short-pants sharpshooters spurn six-guns for cosmic cannon.

Autry and his touring vaudeville troupe rambled into Reading Thursday by bus, trailer and airplane for a one-day stand at the Rajah Theater.

Greeted by Sellout Crowds

Sellout crowds for the two performances indicate that the movie cowboy still is first in the hearts of his young countrymen.

Not only were the kids there, but Pop and Mom, too. Though no official poll was charted, Pop outnumbered Moms, indicating either that Reading mothers are expert at foisting the kids off on Father, or that Pop, too is attracted by the music and twangy slang of the Old West.

Autry's show is a conglomeration of vaudeville (highwire act and bicyclist), music, humor and even some pretty girls, the latter presumably for the fathers in the audience.

Autry, graying at the temples and spreading at the middle, is a typical cowboy-businessman who is going to make it difficult for space heroes to get a solid foot in the cash-box.

This stage-show tour is only one of a dozen Autry activities, all designed to make a cowboy reach trail's end with a full chuck-wagon.

On Road 7½ Weeks

"We've been on the road for about seven and a half weeks, and have about a week and a half to go," Autry noted between performances.

"This enterprise is good for me on several counts. I get a chance to meet my fans, plug my records and movies, and shake hands with my television and radio sponsors. It's also a break in my movie-making activities."

Autry has his own studio in California. In addition to

In all his eight years, Johnny Gosch, 800 Margaret St., Wyomissing Park, never thought this occasion would arrive, when he would be astride Champion, even with Gene Autry in the rumble seat. But here he is, as other members of his West Reading Cub Scout pack crowd close on the stage of the Rajah Theater.—Times Staff Photo.

filming his own television series, he produces films for three other TV shows and has another in the making.

"I've been averaging about six movies a year for theater showing, but I'm kind of sitting back at the moment to see what is going to happen," he observed.

Autry has several full-length movies still unreleased. "I want to see now what's going to happen to Cinemascope and Cinerama. Maybe we'll have to get into that field; maybe we'll have to turn to doing colored films."

Goes on to Baltimore

From Reading, the Autry troupe was moving to Baltimore for a stand today. Most of the cast travels in its own bus; his horses, Champion, and Little Champ, by trailer, and Autry himself in his personal airplane.

With the start he already has on them plus an airplane, how can those space travelers ever hope to catch up with an old cowhand?

Reading Times coverage of Gene Autry's visit to the Rajah on February 18, 1954.

the same bill of fare. The theatre orchestra at this time was conducted by "Saxy" Shollenberger and Joseph Borrelli. Among the entertainers brought in by Keeney were Ethel Waters, Eddie Cantor, George Jessel, Mae West, and Boris Karloff. Many patrons will also remember the Big Bands who came to town. These included the orchestras of Ray Eberle, Lionel Hampton, Sammy Kaye, and the Nat King Cole Trio. Even Gene Autry appeared on the stage of the Rajah. In 1954, Keeney's ad in the January 31 edition of the *Reading Eagle* heralded the visit by the cowboy star as the "Hit Show of 1954," and, indeed, it was. Autry appeared on Thursday, February 18, and in an article written for that Friday's *Reading Times*, staff writer, Dick Peters, told how capacity crowds had turned out to hail the film, radio, and television star. In the article, entitled "Cowboy Here to Stay, Autry Tells Small Fry," Peters stated that a sellout crowd for both performances indicated that "the movie cowboy still is first in the hearts of his young countrymen" with no danger of "the space cadet or rocket ranger" ever replacing him.

The Rajah theatre ceased operation as a motion picture house sometime in the fifties, but it has continued to serve as Reading's center for topnotch stage shows featuring celebrities like Ella Fitzgerald, Betty and Rosemary Clooney, the Three Stooges, Eddie Arnold, and, more recently, Emmy Lou Harris and Shari Lewis (with Lambchops). The North Sixth Street theatre also continues as the home of the Reading Symphony Orchestra, the Star Series, and Haage/Harris Presents programs. Also using its facilities over the years were Reading Civic Opera Company and the Junior League of Reading for its Town Hall Lecture series. In fact, the Rajah Theatre has performed yeoman service as an entertainment center for Reading and is the last of the city's old theatres still in operation. It remains the only old theatre in the city where one can still sit in a velvet seat, gaze dizzily at the domed, frescoed ceiling and the "old world" opulence of the theatre boxes, and reminisce about the old days when Benny Goodman swayed onstage and Gene Autry's horse, Champion, galloped onto the wooden boards. It's still possible to recline in a seat in the gravity-defying balcony and remember sitting there with hordes of other kids during Holy Week watching the free showing of "King of Kings," starring H. B. Warner as a silent Jesus. As of this writing, the possibility exists that the Rajah may be restored to its former glory, enabling it to survive as the last example of Reading's golden age of movie palaces.

Kids flocked to the free showing of "King of Kings" every Easter season at the Rajah. *Reading Eagle* **- March 17, 1948.**

11. THE PLAZA (ORPHEUM)

In his *Annals of the Reading Theatre*, Paul E. Glase relates that ground was broken in 1896 at the site of the former Wilhelm property at 123 - 125 North Fifth Street for the erection of the Masonic Temple. Although the trustees had intended to present concerts, dances, lectures, etc. in the first floor rear hall, they changed their minds when seating was ready and decided to convert the hall into a theatre. Thus, on December 18, 1902, the first floor opened as the Temple Theatre under the management of M. Reis who operated it for two years. Then, in

The Orpheum Theatre at 123 - 125 North Fifth Street in Reading. It became the Plaza in 1946. Courtesy of Ira Bergman.

(Opposite) The Plaza Theatre on North Fifth Street, circa late 1940's.
Photo courtesy of Elmer Quinn.

Reading Eagle ad for the Orpheum, December 10, 1938.

1904, John Mishler leased the house but never opened it. Fortunately, Sidney Wilmer and Walter Vincent arrived on the scene and, after $25,000 worth of renovations, the Orpheum Theatre opened on September 25, 1905, with eight acts of vaudeville. Frank Hill was named manager, while the Orpheum Orchestra played under the direction of J.G.L Schutt. In 1913, dramatic stock was introduced by the operators with a production of "The Fortune Hunter." The stock company would continue for ten successive years before being transferred to the Rajah in 1923 (In 1927, dramatic stock was revived at the North Fifth Street theatre where it remained until 1943).

Wilmer and Vincent operated the Orpheum until 1920 when they subleased it to a Mr. William Masaud who brought in five acts of vaudeville and various silent flicks. Then, as detailed in Mr. Glase's writings, Ben Levin assumed operation of this entertainment center in 1932, bringing in William Heckman as

A stage and screen presentation at the Orpheum Theatre. *Reading Eagle* - April 12, 1945.

Reading Eagle ad of February 22, 1946, announcing the Orpheum's new owner, C.G. Keeney.

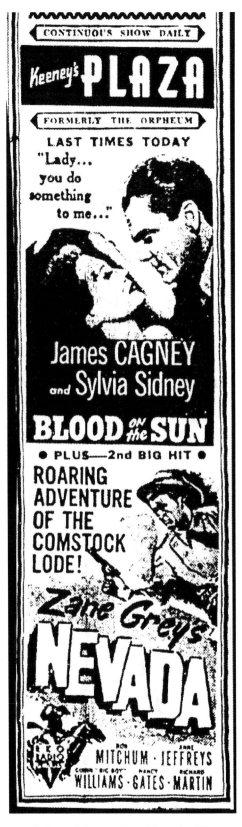

As this ad from the March 18, 1946, edition of the *Reading Eagle* reveals, the Orpheum was now the Plaza.

★PLAZA

SATURDAY MORNING KIDDIE SHOW, 10 A.M.

THE LONE RANGER RIDES AGAIN!

— Wide Screen and Color —

"THE LONE RANGER" PLUS

8 CARTOONS and
RACES -- TOYS

Kids, 25c
Adults, 50c

PLAZA

TODAY ONLY

CONTINUOUS FROM 1 P. M.

KIDS, 10c   ADULTS, 40c

ROY ROGERS

In

"TRAIL OF ROBIN HOOD"

With Rex Allen, Allan "Rocky" Lane, and Monte Hale, in Color.

Also

"STALAG 17"

With William Holden, "The Story of the War's Toughest Prison of War Camp!"

ADDED CARTOON

A Roy Rogers film was featured at the Plaza on February 21, 1954, while the Lone Ranger appeared on the screen on April 19, 1957, a few days before the theatre closed forever *(Reading Eagle)*.

manager. Assisting him was David Brodstein who would become the sole operator around 1936 and continue a program of burlesque and pictures for nine years. In 1946, C.G. Keeney took over the theatre and proceeded to renovate the house, adding a new marquee and changing the name to the Plaza.

Although the ads which appeared in the *Reading Eagle* at the time proclaimed that the theatre was under new management, apparently Mr. Keeney was afraid that loyal patrons of the old theatre might not recognize the new name so he continued to advertise it as the Orpheum for a few months. When the ads finally did appear for the Plaza, they carried the explanatory line "Formerly the Orpheum." When Keeney gave up management of the theatre in the fifties, Max Korr Enterprises, which also operated the Rio, took over its operation. Under both Keeney and Max Korr, the Plaza presented a diversity of programs, including stage shows, burlesque, adult films, and, of course, kiddie shows. It was during this time, in 1948, that the Reading Theatre Guild brought legitimate stage productions back to the location with its opening presentation of "The Barretts of Wimpole Street." The Plaza would remain the home of the guild for the next few years.

Dinnerware was another attraction for women movie patrons. At the Plaza, it was the "World Famous Dresden Duchess Dinnerware" in "22 Karat Gold Trim Service for Six." For a 5¢ service charge, female ticket holders were entitled to a 10" dinner plate, an offer many patrons could not refuse.

But, soon, not even nickel dishware could bring in the crowds as attendance began to wane. Perhaps in a last ditch effort to survive, the Plaza management concocted special programs like the "Giant Marathon Show" which consisted of four "Adults Only" films, with all seats selling for 99¢. Unfortunately, the gimmick failed. The ad in the April 24, 1957, issue of the *Eagle* appears to be the last promotion for the once-popular theatre. If any traces of the Orpheum or Plaza survive, they lie buried beneath a parking lot on North Fifth Street.

★PLAZA TONITE — 4 HITS!
Box Office Opens 6:30 P.M.

TONIGHT ONLY!!
GIANT MARATHON SHOW!
4—BIG HITS—4
ADULTS ONLY—ALL SEATS, 99¢

#1. "HIGH SCHOOL GIRL" | #3. "SHE-DEVIL ISLAND"
#2. "NEARLY 18" | #4. "SINS OF BALI"

The last known ad for the Plaza Theatre. *Reading Eagle* - April 24, 1957.

ASTOR
A WARNER BROS. THEATRE

LAST TWO DAYS
On SCREEN—
"A Midsummer
Night's Dream"
On STAGE—
A Musical Extravaganza
Conducted by
FRED CARDIN

STARTS
FRIDAY!
ENTIRE SHOW
ON SCREEN!

*NO MAN IS LOST
WHILE SOME WOMAN
LOVES HIM!*

ERROL FLYNN
OLIVIA
DeHAVILLAND
The Lovers of "Captain Blood" in

The CHARGE of the LIGHT BRIGADE

Filmed by Warner Bros. from Lord Tennyson's
masterpiece, with a cast of 1000's, including
PATRIC KNOWLES • HENRY
STEPHENSON • NIGEL BRUCE
Donald Crisp • David Niven • Robert
Barrat • Directed by Michael Curtiz

WILMER & VINCENT'S STATE

Now Playing, No Advance in Prices
Nothing Like It Ever Shown Before

An endless array
of fierce, vicious
and ferocious
jungle beasts,
savages and wild
life in the rag-
ged edges of the
world!

RASPIN
PRODUCTIONS
Present

The WILDEST ADVENTURES
EVER FILMED

"EXPLORERS OF THE WORLD"

DIRECTED BY
HAROLD NOICE
Gay Girl Comedy.
"NIAGARA FALLS"

YOU HAVE

*Heard About It!
Read About It!!
Waited for It!!!*

NOW **SEE** IT

Tensely Human . . Packed
with Dramatic Dynamite . .

HOWARD
HUGHES
presents
SCARFACE

UNITED
ARTISTS
PICTURE

"THE SHAME OF A NATION"
With PAUL MUNI, ANN DVORAK,
OSGOOD PERKINS, KAREN MORLEY

LOEW'S
Always Comfortably Cool

WARNER BROS.' COOL THEATRES

ASTOR
ALL WEEK
Greater than in "Sunnyside
Up." Come early—come late
—but don't miss it!
Janet **GAYNOR**
Charles **FARRELL** In
"The First Year"
Added
Fanny Watson Comedy
25c | **35c**
to 1:30 | to 6
P. M. | P. M.

STRAND | GARBO in
Mat., 10c-20c | "As You Desire Me"
Eve., 10c-30c |

Delightfully Cool and Comfortable
Embassy
DIRECTION WILMER & VINCENT

Now Playing
**A WOMAN IS A FOOL
WHO RUNS AWAY
FROM LOVE**

THE MAN FROM YESTERDAY

A Paramount Picture
with
CLAUDETTE
COLBERT
CLIVE
BROOK
CHARLES BOYER
ANDY DEVINE

——EXTRA ADDED——
PARAMOUNT COMEDY
"HIS WEAK END"
With
JOHNNY BURKE

TOM HOWARD
In a Riot of Fun
"Meet the Winner"

STRANGE | PARAMOUNT
AS IT SEEMS | NEWS

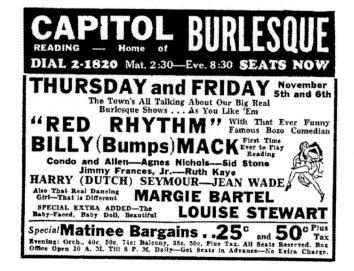

CAPITOL BURLESQUE
READING —— Home of
DIAL 2-1820 Mat. 2:30—Eve. 8:30 **SEATS NOW**

THURSDAY and FRIDAY November 5th and 6th
The Town's All Talking About Our Big Real
Burlesque Shows . . . As You Like 'Em

"RED RHYTHM"
With That Ever Funny
Famous Bozo Comedian
BILLY (Bumps) MACK
First Time
Ever to Play
Reading

Condo and Allen—Agnes Nichols—Sid Stone
Jimmy Frances, Jr.—Ruth Kaye
HARRY (DUTCH) SEYMOUR—JEAN WADE
Also That Real Dancing
Girl—That is Different
MARGIE BARTEL
SPECIAL EXTRA ADDED—The
Baby-Faced, Baby Doll, Beautiful
LOUISE STEWART

Special **Matinee** Bargains . . **25c** and **50c** Plus Tax
Evening: Orch., 40c, 50c, 74c; Balcony, 35c, 50c, Plus Tax. All Seats Reserved. Box
Office Open 10 A. M. Till 8 P. M. Daily—Get Seats in Advance—No Extra Charge.

Reading Eagle ads from 1932 featuring Penn Street movie theatres.

Penn Street movie marquees at night, circa 1942.
Photo courtesy of Ron Romanski.

The Capitol Theatre at 340 Penn Street in Reading, circa 1930's. An Eagle staff writer dubbed it "the splendid half-million dollar picture playhouse" on the day it opened, September 8, 1921.
Photo courtesy of George Meiser, IX.

12. THE CAPITOL

In 1873, the Grand Opera House was erected on the south side of Penn Street below 4th Street. The structure, located above the West Reading Market House, seated approximately 1000 people and was built at a cost of $40,000. During the next four decades, the theatre would undergo various name changes, including "The Family Theatre," C.G. Keeney's "Grand Opera House," and "The Grand Theatre," before the market house was removed and the building remodeled in 1921 to become the Capitol Theatre.

On September 4, 1921, the *Reading Eagle's* page one headline read, "The Capitol Theatre Opens Thursday Afternoon." The text that followed informed readers that "the splendid half-million dollar picture playhouse" contained a $35,000 organ and "many other big features." According to the article, the Capitol, with its 2,000 seats, was the largest in Reading as far as seating capacity. In fact, the writer believed that it would be a long time before the theatre was surpassed in this area "in size, splendor of adornment, or in facilities for entertaining the public 100% returns in amusement value for their admission money." Managing the house, built through the alliance of Wilmer and Vincent and the Stanley Company of America, would be Walter Kantner, with George W. Carr as the resident representative for the Wilmer and Vincent interests. The architects for the building were Hoffman and Henon Company of Philadelphia, while the general contractor was the Pierce-Henon Company, also of the city of brotherly love. However, as the *Eagle* staff writer hastened to point out, whenever possible, local contractors and workman were employed in the building of the theatre which took seventeen months to complete.

It is little wonder the opening of the Capitol rated page one headlines for it was surely a magnificent building. The front contained wide, stained glass windows and a sheet metal and glass marquee on a steel frame. A huge electrical sign ran from the top of the building's center to near the top of the marquee where the theatre's name was worked out in electric lights which flashed brilliantly at night. The ticket seller's booth was in the center of the entrance recess and was, in itself, a work of art in marble,

The opening ad for the Capitol Theatre which opened on September 8, 1921. *Reading Eagle* **- September 7, 1921.**

metal, and polished glass. Five pairs of doors stood behind the booth of the practically fireproof Capitol.

Those who passed through the glass doors on that opening night entered a lobby of polished mirrors and Circassian walnut woodwork with gold trim. The floors were thickly carpeted, with stairways opening off the lobby to the balcony which was also carpeted. Above was a balustraded opening to the mezzanine or promenade floor. To the front of this opening was the manager's office and across the opening was the promenade floor proper which was "comfortably and luxuriously furnished." In addition, a female attendant was always on hand, a feature touted by the writer to be one which "will appeal to the feminine patron from out of town who wishes to rest after the program until a time for another engagement, or until her train or car arrives."

Inside the second set of heavy, glass-panelled doors was the long foyer leading to the theatre proper. At various places along the sides were entrances to stairways, rooms for employees, and retiring rooms. On the walls and ceiling were large beveled mirrors and chandeliers of art glass with designs that filtered light throughout the spaces below. Other features of the foyer and lobby were gold inlays and other decorations of the Italian artists from Philadelphia, making the Capitol, in the writer's words, "a rare assemblage of genius of the decorative art - gorgeous but not gaudy, beautiful without a flaw."

The golden wall tapestries were of velvet and brocade of the heaviest weight while the aisles were heavily carpeted. Approximately 1,200 soft leather seats were on the main floor, while the balcony, boxes, and loge held approximately the same number. In order to give everyone the best possible view of the screen, the center of the main floor was slightly depressed, following the newest idea in seating effects at the time.

The piano sat in an enclosure just below the stage, while the $35,000 manual keyboard organ rested in the wings in the orchestra space. The stage was so large that if the screen were moved, there would be plenty of room for a large theatrical company, along with a huge amount of scenery. Backstage were provisions for ten dressing rooms and high rear lofts for hanging scenery. The Capitol was said to be the first theatre in eastern Pennsylvania to install a modern cooling system. Heating and ventilating were achieved by a system that drew out all of the air in the entire building every few minutes, with fresh filtered air, cooled in summer and warmed in winter, constantly entering to take its place. Radiators sat in the recesses of the walls. The opening film on that September day in 1921 was "The Passion Flower," starring Norma Talmadge. Admission rates were the prices customary in Reading at the time: lower floor - adults, 35¢, children, 17¢; upper floor - adults, 25¢, children, 11¢; boxes and loges were 44¢, with all rates including war taxes.

Paul E. Glase in his *Annals of the Reading Theatre* states that the Capitol, which featured a symphony orchestra and First National motion pictures, had an excellent patronage for the ten years following its opening. However, when more modern theatres were built on Penn Street between Sixth and Eighth, the public turned to them for motion picture entertainment. Thus, when sound came to the Capitol, only a few attractions like "Grand Hotel" and "The Great Ziegfeld" proved popular. Also during this time, Wilmer and Vincent spent a small fortune to equip the theatre with new dressing rooms, stage, and scenery in an attempt to revive vaudeville, but this, too, failed. During the season of 1934 to 1935, stage shows were again attempted with such stars as Ray Bolger, George M. Cohan, and the Earl Carroll Vanities - but with no luck. The once - grand house was then leased to Jack Beck for burlesque and to Walter Finch, who opened a low-price motion picture operation.

This film program continued until approximately January 31, 1943, when what appears to be the last movie ad for the Capitol ran in the local paper. The program, which was advertised as "3--Big Hits--3," featured Robert Stack in "Eagle Squadron," George Raft and Pat O'Brien in "Broadway," and the "Final Thrilling Chapter" of "Dick Tracy vs. Crime Inc." It was also the final chapter for the Capitol as a center for stage and screen entertainment.

For the next few years, the cries of "Bingo" echoed throughout its cavernous auditorium as the sign on the marquee read "Bud's Bingo." Then, in 1948, the old theatre became the Greenfield Furniture store. Later, in the sixties and early seventies, the site was again utilized as a bingo and entertainment center. Sadly, by now the theatre was but a shadow of its former self. In 1975, a wrecking ball demolished the remnants of the once-magnificent Capitol Theatre.

CAPITOL

TODAY
3 -- BIG HITS -- 3

THRILLS - ACTION - SUSPENSE
COMMANDO RAIDS - AIR FIGHTS

ROBERT   DIANA
STACK • BARRYMORE

"EAGLE SQUADRON"

JOHN LODER - JON HALL

2nd Outstanding Feature
MORE EXCITING THAN EVER

GEORGE   PAT
RAFT • O'BRIEN

BROADWAY

JANET BLAIR - BROD CRAWFORD

HIT No. 3
FINAL THRILLING CHAPTER

DICK TRACY vs. CRIME, INC.

The last known Capitol Theatre ad as it appeared in the January 31, 1943, issue of the _Reading Eagle_.

**The Loew's Colonial, circa 1941, when it was host to the MGM hits.
Photo courtesy of Ron Romanski.**

13. THE LOEW'S COLONIAL

The first of the deluxe motion picture houses built "uptown," the Colonial Theatre was erected by Carr and Schad in 1916 on the Breneiser property at 651 - 657 Penn Street between the Ellis Mills store and the Hotel Allen. It opened on April 15, 1917, with the motion picture, "Sleeping Fires," starring Pauline Frederick. The *Reading Eagle* for that day carried an artist's rendition of the new picture house and an article heralding the opening of the $250,000 theatre. Calling the Colonial "one of the finest theatres in the country," the newspaper staff writer went on to explain that Reading's newest film entertainment center was completed only after months of research and a close study of representative theatres in the largest cities in the United States. Moreover, he continued, "patrons will be much delighted with the interior which was designed to impress." One of the biggest features was the Colonial Symphony Orchestra under the direction of Harry E. Fahrbach, organizer and conductor of the Reading Symphony Orchestra. Fittingly for its patrons, the theatre's name was chosen by the "photoplay followers of Reading."

Paul E. Glase relates that the Colonial opened during World War I when lack of fuel and Liberty Bond drives interrupted many performances. But programs at this Reading movie house included the best in motion pictures and, occasionally, stage productions. In fact, hits such as Rudolph Valentino's "The Four Horsemen of the Apocalypse" established early attendance records, perhaps by patrons who were eager for wartime entertainment. Glase states that the most important event at the Colonial occurred on October 21, 1920, when Galli Curci, the celebrated operatic soprano, appeared in concert. Front row seats sold for $5 and loge seats for $10, a fortune for most people during those years. However, the event was a huge success, with crowds lining the curbs to catch a glimpse of the fashionable audience. The Carr and Schad firm also produced Reading's only newsreel, entitled "Community Events," for more than ten years, capturing all of the important events around the city and county. The managers for the first few years were Mike Carmen, Harry Stimmel, and Clarence Latshaw, with Alfred Seward and Robert E. Henke as organists.

On September 21, 1925, the MGM lion came roaring into the Colonial when Loew's Incorporated purchased the building from Carr and Schad who moved to the Arcadia location in the 700 block of Penn Street. Glase relates that there was no interruption in the operation as the old firm closed on Saturday evening and the new firm opened Monday. Feature pictures and occasional stage appear-

The early days of the Colonial Theatre which opened on April 15, 1917.
Photo courtesy of John Glase.

ances remained as the usual programs at the new MGM Loew's. Also retained was Harry E. Fahrbach as the orchestra director and Robert E. Henke as organist, with Mabel E. Stoudt as relief organist. The *Reading Eagle* on that opening day in September advertised the program for the Loew's as featuring the motion picture, "Ever the Twain Shall Meet," along with the Loew's Colonial Concert Orchestra performing the overture, "The Life of Stephen Foster." There were also short features, a stage attraction, and a novelty number by organist Henke. In July of 1926, a $50,000 Wurlitzer Pipe Organ was installed, and, later that year, a new cooling system. Sound equipment came to the Loew's in 1929. Managers during those early years included Larry Jacobs, Howard Foerste, Livingstone Lanning, and Robert Suits.

On January 14, 1932, child actor Jackie Cooper made a personal appearance at the theatre whose management brought in as their guests not only the children from Reading's poor families but also the youngsters from St. Catherine's Orphanage and other institutions. In all, 1800 children attended the performance. Eddie Cantor was another visitor to the Loew's during the thirties, as were many other stars. On February 18, 1935, the first dawn showing of a film in Reading occurred at this Penn Street theatre when the management initiated a 6:30 A.M. breakfast show which featured free coffee and donuts to patrons who wished to catch a picture before heading off to work or after finishing a tour on the night shift. Ironically, the first breakfast show featured a Clark Gable film entitled, "After Office Hours." The decade of the thirties also witnessed a price reduction at this movie house as prices plummeted to 25¢ for adults and 15¢ for children who attended the Friday matinees. Evening performances were 40¢ and 15¢, respectively, with balcony seats costing 25¢.

Artist's sketch of the new Colonial Theatre which opened in 1917 as the first "deluxe" theatre uptown.
Reading Eagle - April 15, 1917.

Reading Eagle ad for the opening of Carr & Schad's Colonial on April 15, 1917.

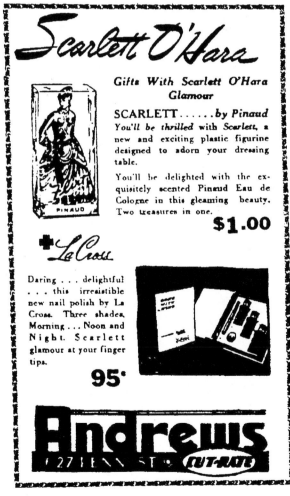

Reading Eagle ads highlighting Reading's celebration of the premiere of "Gone With The Wind" which opened at the Loew's on December 21, 1939.

In 1939 came the startling news that Reading, Pennsylvania, had been chosen as one of a few select cities in the country to premier David O. Selznick's much-heralded epic motion picture, "Gone With the Wind." As the December 11 edition of the *Reading Eagle* announced, "GWTW" would be launched in seven key cities that month - New York, Los Angeles, Boston, Atlanta, Cincinnati, Houston, and Reading. This multiple Academy Award - winning film opened in Reading on December 21, 1939, at the Loew's Theatre and ran for four record-breaking weeks. As the ad campaign trumpeted, Reading

September 15, 1943, *Reading Eagle* ad for one of MGM's patriotic films. Patrons were urged to buy war bonds.

welcomed the film "with open arms." W.T. Grant's featured "GWTW" prints which women could use to sew copies of their favorite dresses from the film. This five-and-dime also sold "Gone With the Wind" scarves. At the American House at Fourth and Penn, patrons were treated to "Plantation Days," a program of Southern music inspired by the film. Shoppers at the upscale Jeannette Shop were entertained with an exclusive showing of "authentic reproductions of the original 'GWTW' gowns." Andrews Cutrate featured an "exciting plastic figurine" of Scarlett for the ladies' dressing tables and an "irresistible new nail polish" to put Scarlett's glamour on every woman's fingertips. For the chocoholics, People's Service Store featured "GWTW" chocolates for $1.50 a pound, and a local car dealer promised that the cars he sold were so fast that anyone buying one would be "gone with the wind." Those were an exciting four weeks for Readingites. Bertrand Mellinger, chief projectionist at the Loew's from 1927 to 1963, remarked in an article written for the *Sunday Eagle Magazine* of August 20, 1961, that he had shown this major motion picture so many times, he almost memorized the script.

The forties brought war and with it came the bond drives so familiar to those who patronized the movie theatres during those days. Of course, World War II had to come to the movies and it did in such films as "Flying Tigers," "The Purple Heart," and MGM's "Salute to the Marines" which played the Loew's on September 15, 1943. With these films came the reminders to all patriotic Americans to "Back the Attack - Buy War Bonds." Along with the city's other theatres, the Loew's participated in various parades, drives, and rallies which supported the war. Near the end of World War II, on August 1, 1941, Larry Levy succeeded W. Brock Whitlock as manager of this movie palace.

The forties was also the decade when MGM produced their extravagant technicolor musicals, featuring such stars as Judy Garland, Gene Kelly, Fred Astaire, Jane Powell, Mickey Rooney, Esther Williams, and so many others that no one questioned Louis B. Mayer's statement that the studio had "more stars than there are in the heavens." And they all played the Loew's. In addition to the motion pictures, the theatre during these years featured special programs and contests for its patrons. For example, on July 19, 1946, the boy and girl finalists from the city's playgrounds competed on the Loew's stage for the "freckles crown." In 1948, the theatre was pleased to announce that Reading's Bicentennial Queen, Miss Marie E. Henne, would be attending the press review showing of the film, "State of the Union," at the Loew's Capitol Theatre in Washington, D.C. Also that year, the publicity department for the local theatre claimed in a *Reading Eagle* ad that the cops at Seventh and Penn were astounded by the crowds of people blocking traffic as they lined up to see Judy Garland and Fred Astaire in the holiday hit, "Easter Parade." Another promotion during the glory days of the Loew's involved the March of Dimes campaign in which jars containing names of the various Berks County communities were set up on tables outside the theatre. Patrons' dimes were to be put into the jars which represented their particular communities in an effort to help that area be victorious in collecting the most money for the cause.

Larry Levy managed the Loew's into the fifties when attendance began to drop. But the early years of that decade still brought crowds, especially teenage girls who crowded the theatre anytime a film was shown which featured their heroine, Esther Williams, rising from the MGM-blue water like Neptune's daughter, waving a wand of sparkling light. The management at this time also tried revivals of earlier films like 1935's "Mutiny on the Bounty" and 1937's "A Day at the Races." Robert Diem took over the operation in 1956 and continued as manager until March of 1963 when the lease with the Loew's corporation expired, and the movie palace was leased to the Stanley Warner Corporation, becoming known as "Stanley Warner's Colonial." The new manager, Bert Leighton, who had managed the Warner in the 700 block of Penn Street, considered it a good move since the Loew's auditorium contained 1,700 seats as compared to the Warner's 1,150. However, Robert Diem did not see much future in the old movie house since he felt that Reading had too many theatres for the limited amount of pa-

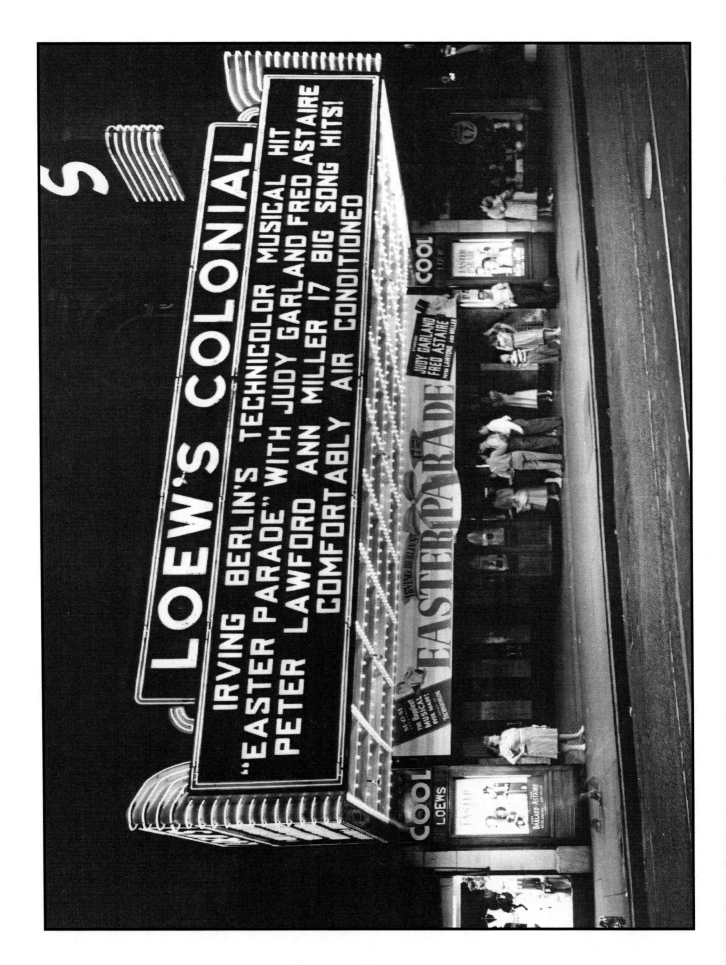

'GOSH! AN EASTER PARADE IN JULY!"

That's what the cops at 7th and Penn Streets are saying as crowds of people block traffic at Loew's. New records! New box office lines never before witnessed in the theatre's history!

MGM Presents
IRVING BERLIN'S
"EASTER PARADE"
In Color by Technicolor
JUDY GARLAND — FRED ASTAIRE
PETER LAWFORD — ANN MILLER

Now Showing
AIR CONDITIONED
LOEW'S

Crowds line the sidewalk in front of the Loew's waiting to buy tickets for the MGM hit, "Easter Parade."
Reading Eagle - July 25, 1948.

This *Reading Eagle* ad of April 6, 1948, publicized Reading's Bicentennial Queen's visit to Loew's Colonial in Washington.

LOEW'S THEATRE

Announces With Pleasure That

Reading's Bicentennial Queen

MISS MARIE E. HENNE

Will attend the Press Review showing sponsored by the White House Correspondents' Association of Metro-Goldwyn-Mayer and Liberty Film's

"STATE OF THE UNION"

Produced and Directed by Frank Capra and Starring

SPENCER	KATHARINE	VAN
TRACY	**HEPBURN**	**JOHNSON**

At LOEW'S CAPITOL Theatre, Washington, D. C.

WEDNESDAY EVENING, APRIL SEVENTH

(Opposite) "Easter Parade" comes to the Loew's in 1948.
Photo courtesy of Ron Romanski.

Robert Taylor and Esther Williams between shows at the Loew's Theatre sometime in the late 1940's. In the background on the left is Larry McDermott of the *Reading Eagle* staff and on the right is Larry Levy, manager of the Loew's. Photo courtesy of Ed Foley, a former projectionist & theatre manager.

Loew's *Reading Eagle* ad for June 26, 1949, featuring a film starring Esther Williams who was every young girl's heroine.

tronage and the number of good motion pictures available.

For approximately the next five years, Warner operated the former Loew's, but the days of the glorious MGM technicolor movies were gone. Gone also were the lines which used to stretch for a block down Penn Street. In 1968, Marshall and Roed tried to revive the Colonial, but by the year it was torn down, 1970, the name on the marquee read, "James Maurer Colonial." Maurer had operated the theatre for a few months in 1969 before closing it for good.

The article in the *Reading Eagle* on March 18, 1970, detailing the demolition of the once-magnificent movie house was entitled "Not 'West Side Story' But More Like 'Gone With the Wind.'" The old theatre came tumbling down to make way for the Penn Street Mall. Accompanying the article were two photos of the rubble left behind by the destruction of Reading's first deluxe uptown movie palace. With a few swings of the "grim wrecker's" ball, the Loew's was truly "gone with the wind."

**Bertrand Mellinger, chief projectionist at the Loew's from 1927 - 1963.
Photo courtesy of Donald Mellinger.**

**The Stanley Warner Colonial as seen on October 27, 1963, after being taken over by the management of the former Warner Theatre.
Photo courtesy of the Reading Redevelopment Authority.**

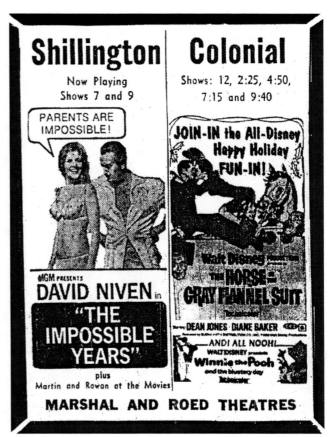

Reading Eagle ad for December 30, 1968, when Marshal & Roed took over the Shillington and the Loew's.

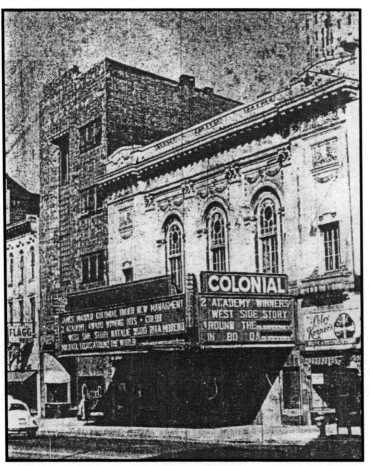

James Maurer's Colonial Theatre shortly before being torn down in 1970. *Reading Eagle* - March 18, 1970.

Not 'West Side Story' But More Like 'Gone With the Wind'

"West Side Story" was the last show to get top billing at the Colonial Theater in Downtown East. The movie house on the north side of Penn street south of the Berks County courthouse (top right corner of top left photo) will come tumbling down to make room for Penn Mall. The Reading Redevelopment Authority is demolishing several buildings in the 7th and Penn streets area. The picture above shows the rear of a former furniture store adjacent to the theater that has to be razed before the theater. Directly below is another view of the rear of the former furniture store and at the bottom is a view of the rear of the theater and the former store. — Eagle Photos by Richard T. Miller.

Reading Eagle coverage of the demolition of the Loew's Colonial Theatre, March 18, 1970.

Embassy Theatre Opens Today

Premiere . Performance at 7 P. M. Will Be Preceded by Hour of Public Inspection.

Reading's latest playhouse, the Embassy Theatre, on Penn street between Seventh and Eighth, is completed and ready for its formal opening this evening. Working day and night craftsmen put the finishing touches to the newest addition of Wilmer & Vincent's chain, which will be the 26th operated in seven cities in the East.

Both Sidney Wilmer and Walter Vincent will attend the gala opening this evening, which will be preceded by an hour of public inspection. There will be no glitter and glamor attendant with the opening. A bugler from Haag Post, Veterans of Foreign Wars, will sound reveille and 15 members of all the posts of the V. F. W. will hoist two American flags in the front of the theatre.

Two Shows Tonight.

With its glittering front of gold and white terra cotta outlined in neon lights, the bright chromium doors of the Embassy will swing open at 6 o'clock tonight for inspection. Two showing, starting at 7 and 9, will follow.

All day yesterday and far into the morning workmen put the finishing touches to the theatre—cleaning, adjusting projectors and sound apparatus and installing the last pieces of furniture.

"We're all ready to dazzle the eyes of Reading and Berks theatregoers," A. Frank O'Brien, manager, said. "Both of the owners of our chain saw the theatre this afternoon and they agreed that there is probably nothing in America quite like this amusement house. We saw a marvelous picture palace when we viewed the plans many months ago, but, the actual theatre is far, far beyond anything we expected."

Standing out in the vari-colored furnishings are those to which modern art has shown particular favor—black, silver, gold. Silver shines from the walls and the grilled sides of the room. It gleams from a gate, which opens and closes before the screen; in railings, in display boxes, in the lobby entrance, and in the ticket booth. Added to these hues are sky blue, which tints the vaulted ceiling; red, bronze, orange, and green, which color the walls.

2,000 Seats in Theatre.

Even the 2,000 seats lend a hand in multi-color effect with their bright shades of red and yellow. Then there's a green terrace sloping from the front of the auditorium to the screen, and trees and shrubbery in back of the screen.

"First-nighters" will not sit through a dedicatory address. After the ceremony in front of the theatre the national anthem will be played on the sound equipment.

Preceding the chief attraction, "Stolen Heaven," in which Nancy Carroll and Phillips Holmes are featured, will be a short subject, including Paramount Sound News, "Tigers of the Deep," a sportlight, and a cartoon novelty, "The Radio Racket." The same bill will be shown on the Embassy's screen throughout the week.

A. Frank O'Brien, district manager for the Wilmer & Vincent circuit in this city and who will direct the affairs at the new Embassy, has been with the firm longer than any other individual in their employ. He began as assistant treasurer at Utica, N. Y., in 1902. In 1905 he was made treasurer of the Orpheum, this city, and was a member of the popular Wilmer & Vincent staff, at that time headed by Frank D. Hill, manager; John J. Murphy, musical director, and James Van Reed, assistant treasurer. From Reading he went to Allentown, and then New York, returning to this city last Fall.

O'Brien will move into his new office in the Embassy Theatre building within the next week.

Directing the construction of the theatre was Herman Nowitsky, chief construction engineer for Wilmer & Vincent. He has been with these men since 1907 designing stage effects, creating lighting effects, in addition to employing his expert knowledge of engineering to construction of new theatres. He has made a host of friends here. His home is in Norfolk, Va.

In addition to the State, Capitol and Rajah in Reading, with a lease on the Orpheum, Wilmer & Vincent operate theatres in Easton, Allentown, Harrisburg, Altoona, Richmond and Norfolk, Va.

NEW HOME OF WILMER & VINCENT'S EMBASSY THEATRE

Reading Eagle coverage of the opening of the Embassy Theatre, April 4, 1931.

75

14. THE EMBASSY

As readers of the *Reading Eagle* opened their newspapers on April 4, 1931, they were greeted with the announcement that Reading's newest theatre would be premiering that evening with a 7 P.M. showing of "Stolen Heaven," featuring Nancy Carrol. Built by Sidney Wilmer and Walter Vincent, who would be attending the opening along with other dignitaries, this "million dollar house" would be the largest theatre in Reading with 2,460 seats. The theatre was constructed on properties owned by Ad. and Samuel Kutz and E.I. Kaufmann and had once been the site of the Berks County Court House and Bubp Grocery store. Built by Charles Schlegel and Son and designed by William H. Lee, this magnificent ediface was to be called "The Hollywood" but, for some unknown reason, the name was changed before the opening. Paul E. Glase recalls in his *Annals of the Reading Theatre* that the Haage Post Drum and Bugle Corps began the opening ceremonies by sounding reveille after which the veterans of the Hunter Liggett and Greater Reading Posts hoisted the colors. Then the audience sang the national anthem and the Embassy officially opened. And what an audience it must have been as 8,000 first nighters crowded 745 Penn Street in an attempt to be the first to view the splendor! Since the theatre's capacity was reached within minutes of the opening, 4,000 patrons spent an hour touring the house before the early show, according to the edition of the *Reading Eagle* which hit the streets the day after the theatre's premiere. In addition, nearly as many patrons filled the foyer and lined Penn Street waiting for the second show. The wait was worth it, for those first nighters were treated to an overwhelming sight as they entered Reading's newest motion picture palace.

Paul Glase states that the Embassy was designed to carry out an atmospheric theme with ornamental decorations such as winged unicorns, chromium doors, balustrades and lighting fixtures, and display frames inlaid with black Italian marble. The *Reading Eagle* described a modernistic entrance with two-tone cement connecting with terrazzo borders. The vestibule was inlaid with rubber tile of assorted colors while massive aluminum doors banked the lobby whose walls were of black marble with aluminum trimmings. The artistic lobby display frames were of shadow box design. Ceiling mural paintings depicted the spirit of the motion picture - the newsreel, romance, comedy, and adventure. Easy stairways in the foyer led to the lounges, loges, and balcony. The lounge was elaborately furnished and surrounded with ladies' rest rooms, men's smoking rooms, public telephones, and a large check room. The main auditorium, claimed the *Eagle* staff writer, was similar to an ampitheatre of old with the curving ceiling making a graceful sweep

Artist's drawing of the proposed 3000 seat Hollywood Theatre which became the Embassy. *Reading Eagle* **- July 30, 1930.**

Paul E. Glase and employees posing for a film promotional in front of the Embassy Theatre, circa 1938. Standing to the right of the sign are, left to right, usherettes Verna (Brunner) Keiser, unidentified usherette, Vera (Reidel) Wennell, and Alice Koble. Next to them are doorman Jimmy Moyer, bookkeeper Hazel John, Al Hostler, manager of the State Theatre, and Paul E. Glase. Others are unidentified.

Photo courtesy of Vera (Reidel) Wennell of Lincoln Park.

Reception for Thomas Leinbach held in the Embassy Theatre on November 7, 1938. The Embassy staff is in the background on the steps.

Photo courtesy of Vera (Reidel) Wennell.

from one end of the auditorium to the other. In addition, the ceiling reflected the sky-blue hue of the heavens. Eugene Plank, who managed the theatre at the time of its disastrous fire, recalled that tiny electric stars once flickered in the ceiling and engineers had tried to perfect a cloud effect, using steam. However, the clouds evaporated and water droplets fell on surprised patrons.

Since the Embassy was designed primarily for screen entertainment, it was built without a stage. Instead, there was a green terrace flanked by huge, ornamental gates weighing several tons. Draperies and curtains were absent and the whole effect was one of a Grecian Garden with a terraced lawn stretching from the floor of the auditorium to the screen which offset the receding sky. The terrace was flanked by trees, shrubbery, fountains and columns, all designed with a modernistic touch. The screen was the latest and the largest designed for sound films while the booth contained the newest type of Western Electric equipment. Modernistic speakers were designed to reproduce the speaking and singing voice with a quality as fine as the best symphony orchestra. Patrons throughout the theatre sat in spring cushion opera chairs similar to those found in the loge sections of the Roxy and Mayfair in New York City. The carpeting in the Embassy was also modernistic and the heating and cooling plants were the latest in scientific systems. Everything operated electrically and was designed to be converted with ease to meet every requirement of the future (talkies, television, stage productions, etc). For the convenience of patrons, there was a unit of girl ushers, a nurse in the lounge, and a footman who arranged to have autos checked and driven to a nearby parking garage to avoid parking inconveniences. Theatre phones were also installed for the benefit of hearing impaired theatregoers. Those worried about safety could feel secure in the knowledge that this motion picture house was built with sufficient exits to vacate the building in two minutes if the need arose.

Frank O'Brien, the district manager for the Wilmer and Vincent circuit in Reading, was put in charge of the Embassy's affairs. O'Brien managed the Embassy for two years until Paul E. Glase became resident manager in 1933. Although the theatre was designed for motion pictures, various stars did make appearances. Elmer Quinn, who sometimes played in the house orchestra, recalls that the management would remove the first seven rows of seats in order to make room for these presentations. Thus, on February 7, 1935, the Embassy played host to Amos and Andy and on January 25, 1940, Gene Autry rode in on Champion, the Wonder Horse. In 1944, the Wilmer and Vincent chain joined the Fabian Theatre Company which operated sixty-five theatres in New York and would now operate the Ritz and Penn in addition to the Embassy.

Glase, as manager of this "million dollar picture house," later to be called "the Queen,"

THEATRE MANAGERS ACTIVE IN WAR BOND CAMPAIGNS 1942 - 1946
(Standing left to right) Henry Sork, Samuel Felt, Howard H. Whittle, Emmanuel Rosenberg, Paul E. Glase, Harry Friedland, John Leiss, George F. Gross, Joseph Shverha, Paul H. Estely, J. Lester Stallman, James F. Moyer.

(Seated) C.G. Keeney, A. Birk Binnard, Lawrence Levy, David J. Hill, Executive Director Berks County War Finance Committee, Nat Silver, H.J. Schad.

Photo from Paul E. Glase's _Annals of the Reading Theatre._

brought many special attractions to wartime Reading. For example, in 1943, he staged a military parade as part of the publicity for the film, "Crash Dive." This event was held in conjunction with a local recruiting drive for World War II and was one of many events sponsored by the management of the local theatres in an attempt to boost the war effort. Mr. Glase also arranged war bond drives and sales and joined with eleven other Reading theatres in an "entertainment for scrap" trade which gave a free movie ticket to patrons for every three pounds of scrap turned in. War bonds and stamps were also sold in every theatre lobby. For one of these joint promotions, Reading's movie theatre operators placed effigies of Hitler, Mussollini, and Hirohito in an old jalopy and parked it at the top of Penn Street near City Park. As people bought bonds, they were entitled to give the car a push down the street. The goal was to sell enough bonds to eventually shove the car and its occupants to the foot of Penn Street and into the Schuylkill. The drive was a huge success as Hitler and friends "drowned" in the black silt of the river. Another special event during Glase's tenure occurred in 1948 in honor of Reading's Bicentennial when a special short film shot entirely in Reading and entitled, "My Home Town," was shown at the Embassy. The film was narrated by Bill Stern.

Paul E. Glase ran the Queen successfully until 1954 when Eugene Plank took over its operation. Those who worked for Glase remember him as a wonderful boss. Vera (Reidel) Wennel, who worked as an usherette at the theatre, recalls the parties that Peg Glase held for his employees, sending them an invitation in the form of a summons. Paul Glase passed away on September 22, 1955, leaving a great void for not only his family but also Reading in general, especially the theatre community. Fortunately,

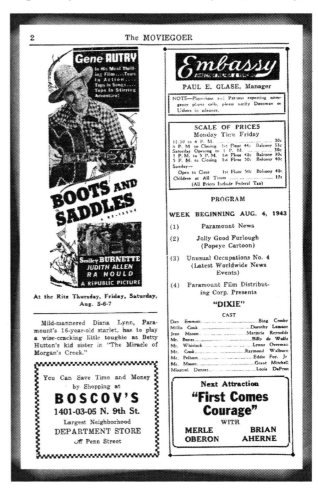

Theatre ads from Wilmer & Vincent's _Moviegoer_, August 4, 1943, edition.

he left a legacy in the form of voluminous scrapbooks chronicling the history of the theatre in Reading. Were it not for his writings and collections, an important part of Reading's past would be lost.

Eugene Plank came on the scene in 1954, a time when the movie industry was reeling from the effects of television's knockout punch. Incidentally, it was Plank who convinced Peg Glase to hire male ushers at the Embassy. In Hollywood, those in charge of film production were fighting back by coming up with special film techniques aimed at regaining straying audiences. Among those gimmicks were 3-D, CinemaScope, VistaVision, Todd-A-O, Stereo Sound, and Cinerama. The first CinemaScope film, "The Robe," was released by the studios in 1953. It ran for six weeks at the Embassy. On December 29, 1954, one of the last big Hollywood musicals, Irving Berlin's "There's No Business Like Show Business," played the Embassy in an attempt to bring patrons to the theatre. It, too, was filmed in CinemaScope and was the Queen's salute to the New Year of 1955. The staff of the Embassy brought in 1956 by staging a New Year's Eve kiddies' matinee party which featured "Our Gang" comedies, cartoons, an "action western hit," and free oranges, peanut butter cups, soda, and "noisemakers for all."

Eugene Plank managed the Embassy for sixteen years, up until the time of the ruinous March fire of 1970 which closed the doors of the Queen forever. According to the article written by Charles M. Gallagher of the *Reading Eagle* for the March 16 edition, the fire which gutted this Penn Street movie palace was discovered at 4:15 A.M. by Patrolman Earl Krow who called in the alarm. The raging inferno, which was later termed suspicious, was not brought under control until 6 A.M. Apparently started at the rear of the stage, the fire spread quickly to the ceiling tapestries which then dropped onto the seats, setting them on fire. When the conflagration was finally out, the entire theatre was inundated with water. Ironically, on April 1, 1970, the Embassy was to be taken over by Paul J. Angstadt and Richard C. Wolfe, managers of the Strand Theatre which had been damaged similarly only a month before.

According to Gallagher's article, Plank remembered his days at the Embassy with great fondness, recalling the richness of variety in the old-time theatre programs. At one time, Plank related, the only snacks offered in movie houses were candy bars, thus the reason for nearby soda fountains, candy stores, and luncheonettes. In fact, many of these establishments were built next door to the theatres so that patrons could grab a bite to eat before or after the show. Even though attendance was down, Plank felt

July 18, 1948, *Reading Eagle* ad for the Embassy which was then showing the film "My Home Town" featuring the city of Reading.

that the Embassy was still enjoying some good times in recent years, with the biggest crowds on Friday and Saturday evenings and Sunday afternoons. In particular, the manager remembered the film, "The Molly Maguires," as bringing in good crowds. In fact, it was necessary to open the balcony in order to accommodate the patrons. The James Bond movies were also popular with audiences in the last two decades before the fire, with the largest grosser being "Thunder Ball." Plank was convinced that the fire was deliberately set since it started in the sound stage area where it couldn't be seen from Penn Street and could gain the greatest headway before being detected. In addition, firemen discovered that a side door had been propped open with a ladder.

Eugene Plank was slated at the time to become the manager of the new movie theatre opening in the Berkshire Mall, a film house with 850 seats compared to the Embassy's 2,460. As for the Queen, like most of the other Penn Street theatres, she was scheduled to be demolished within the next two years to make way for the Penn Street Mall. However, Plank told Gallagher that he left with a tear in his eye for he never thought that "the Queen would die this way." In 1972, after another fire, she was torn down. No mall was ever built and, at the time of this writing, the site is a parking lot.

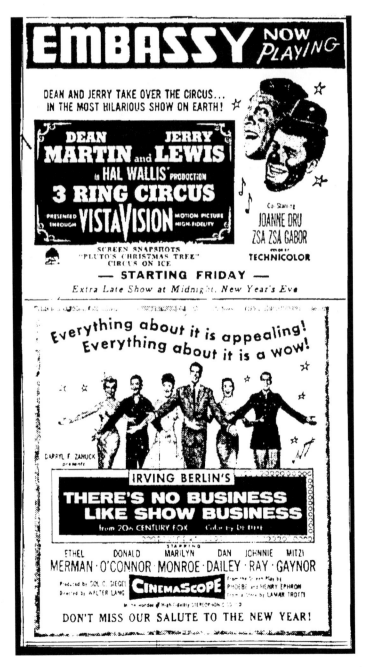

Hollywood fights back with VistaVision and CinemaScope. *Reading Eagle* - December 29, 1954.

The Embassy's New Year's Eve party for the kids. *Reading Eagle* - December 30, 1955.

The Embassy Theatre, circa 1956, showcasing Elvis Presley's first motion picture, "Love Me Tender."
Photo courtesy of John Glase.

The Embassy Theatre on a rainy night in 1958. What had once been the Embassy Sweet Shop and, later, Lechleitner's Candy Shop, has become Ralph's Nut and Candy Shop. Photo courtesy of Elmer Quinn.

Paul E. Glase Dies In Reading Hospital

PAUL E. GLASE

Manager of Embassy, Aged 71, Was Versed In Theatrical History

Paul E. Glase, 71, manager of the Embassy Theater and nationally recognized authority on the history of entertainment, died in the Reading Hospital this morning where he had been a medical patient since last Friday.

Glase was probably best known for his collection of theater programs and playbills which he kept at his home, 1406 E. Wyomissing Blvd.

His collection is believed to be the largest private one of its kind in the world and included 75,000 items, according to his own estimate, in 1948. Some of the English playbills he acquired predated the American stage.

Had Movies in Collection

His collection also contains other items connected with entertainment. He had more than 1,000 books on stage, screen, radio, concert and circus fields. He also had old single reel movies in his collection and a complete list of vaudeville acts that played here since 1905.

Reading Eagle coverage of the death of Paul E. Glase.

A view of the Embassy's interior in a photo taken by John Glase. Courtesy of John Glase.

A side view which illustrates the immensity of the Embassy Theatre building. Photo courtesy of the Reading Redevelopment Authority.

READING EAGLE

WEEU
850
ON YOUR RADIO

News, Weather
On the Hour
And Half-Hour

PAGE NINETEEN   SECOND SECTION

MONDAY, MARCH 16, 1970

Fire Is a Tragic Game in Town

The film title on the marque of the Embassy seems a macabre jest to firemen who were called out to quell the second theater fire in Reading in the past month. —Eagle Photos.

Reading Eagle coverage of the March 16, 1970, fire which destroyed the Embassy. Also following page.

Embassy Theater's Seats Ruined by Blaze

A fireman stands inside the Embassy Theater, 745 Penn St., this morning and scans the charred and burned seats, the result of a fire which spread from the stage area to ceiling tapestry which fell to the seats. This morning's two-alarm fire was the second major theater blaze to occur in Reading within four weeks. Additional photos on Page 19.—Eagle Photo by Richard T. Miller.

Eugene Plank, manager of the Embassy Theatre, bids farewell to his beloved "Queen."
Photo courtesy of the Reading Eagle / Times.

The State Theatre at 755 Penn Street. It became the Warner in 1941.
Photo courtesy of John Glase.

Store front advertising for local radio programs featuring Robert E. Henke at the console of the State's organ.
Photo courtesy of John Glase.

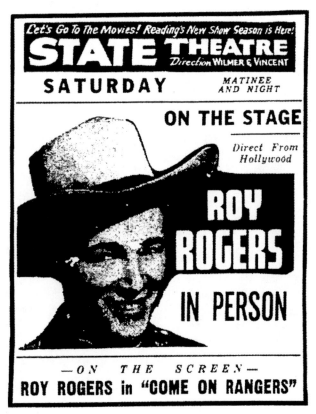

Roy Rogers visits the State.
Reading Eagle Ad - December 9, 1938.

15. The Warner (State)

By the time Roy Rogers made an appearance on the stage of the State Theatre at 755 Penn Street on December 9, 1938, the theatre had been operating for thirteen years under that banner, for it was on October 11, 1925, that the *Reading Eagle* headline read "State's Opening Draws Capacity Crowd." What had once been the site of the Hippodrome Theatre became the State on that date under the management of Wilmer and Vincent. After two weeks of decorating and reconstruction, this new home of Paramount Pictures was proclaimed to be "well-deserving of the title, 'The Theatre Beautiful.' " As the crowds filled the house on that October evening to see the motion picture, "The Man Who Found Himself," with Thomas Meigham, they were treated to the sounds of "The William Tell Overture" as performed by the fifteen-piece house orchestra.

In 1931, Wilmer and Vincent leased the theatre to Emory and Jones, but took back control in 1932 after an unsuccessful season. They would continue at the helm until 1941 when Warner Brothers leased the building. However, it was Wilmer and Vincent who initiated the State's family policy by featuring children's and newsboys' parties, Sunday night radio broadcasts by Reading artists in concert programs, and children's community sings by special arrangement with local radio stations. Stations WRAW and WEEU also broadcast Robert E. Henke playing request numbers at the console of the State's organ. Donald Mellinger of Wernersville, whose father was chief projectionist at the Loew's Theatre for many years, remembers that the State featured many cowboy films during its glory days. Apparently, these films were capable of stirring audiences to great emotional heights, for Mellinger recalls being in the audience one evening and witnessing a woman jumping out of her seat and shouting, "Look out behind you!" to the hero who was about to be ambushed by the villain.

Paul Glase writes that in 1941, Warner Brothers leased the theatre and proceeded to make elaborate renovations which included a new marquee, box office, lobby, rest rooms, and smoking room. In fact, the April 11, 1941, edition of the *Reading Eagle* hailed the theatre as "the last word in theatre construction,... its beauty and appointments... a fitting contribution to the expansion and growth of Reading." In addition, declared the ad writer, patrons could "always be assured of courtesy, service, warm hospitality, and the best of entertainment in this new Warner Theatre. From its impressive entrance, which sparkles like a diamond with its myriad lights and its fascinating polar design, to its soft, caressing interior, to its scientific air conditioning, the Warner Theatre embraces modernism in all its far-reaching form."

The renovation of the 1,228 seat Warner, which opened on April 12, 1941, with Bette Davis in "The Great

Gala OPENING
WARNER BROS.
New AIR-CONDITIONED
WARNER
THEATRE
755 PENN STREET, READING, PA.
TOMORROW
Saturday, April 12th
DOORS OPEN 12 NOON
OPENING ATTRACTION
Warner Bros. Great Hit!
"HE'S MINE...
'TIL HE LEARNS
THE TRUTH
ABOUT ME"
BETTE
DAVIS
IN
THE GREAT LIE

Reading Eagle ad of April 11, 1941, which announced the opening of the Warner Theatre (formerly the State.)

**The Warner Theatre, circa 1948.
Photo courtesy of Elmer Quinn.**

Lie," had cost its new management $75,000. But it was worth the price, for over the years which were to follow, the Warner gained a reputation for extended runs of motion pictures. In fact, the theatre set new records with films like "Sergeant York" and "Casablanca," which ran for six weeks. In addition, the Warner participated in the numerous World War II bond drives and other money-raising efforts by featuring special showings which benefited various organizations. One example was the August 24, 1943, running of Irving Berlin's morale booster, "This Is the Army." This motion picture, which featured a stirring rendition of "God Bless America" by a young Kate Smith, raised money for the Army Emergency Relief Fund. According to the *Reading Eagle* volume, *Reading Newsweek-Volume One*, the benefit was a huge success with local audiences for there were few vacant seats at this showing where ticket prices ranged from two to ten dollars.

In the fifties, new technology came to the Warner in the form of the first 3-D motion picture, "B-Wani Devil," released in 1953. Lee Kline, chief projectionist at the theatre at the time, recollected in "Film Projectionists Recall the Early Talkies Here," an article which appeared in the August 20, 1961, edition of the *Sunday Eagle Magazine*, that he was one of the first to experience problems with 3-D movies. He explained that in order to project the image, the projectionist had to keep two projectors running at the same time. However, if one ran slightly faster than the other, the picture would blur. In addition, if the film broke, the depth effect was lost. Kline remembered that the reels were quite heavy and large, making them hard to handle.

On January 21, 1954, the Warner screened the CinemaScope film, "The Robe," which also played the Embassy. As the advertisement which appeared in the *Reading Eagle* on that day proclaimed, the newest-in-technology film introduced an "Anamorphic Lens Process on the newly-created curved, Miracle Mirror Screen" which "achieves life-like realism and depth." In addition, the movie gave audiences "The magic of Stereophonic Sound."

Stanley Warner Corporation bought the Warner in 1955 and attempted to hang on for the next eight years by showing a variety of films catering to an audience becoming increasingly sophisticated, thanks in large part to television. In 1958, "Auntie Mame," a sophisticate in her own right, and played by Rosalind Russell, tried to lure audiences to the theatre's midnight New Year's Eve show. She was fairly successful, but musicals were becoming a dying breed. It was also during these years that Reading's first-run houses began showing double feature programs, a practice which had been mostly confined to the second-run theatres. As a January 9, 1960, *Reading Eagle* ad seems to demonstrate, the cowboy was still popular. Playing side-by-side at the Warner that day were two westerns, "Ride Lonesome," with Randolph Scott, and "The Young Land" (which promised "young blood racing" and "young loves raging"). Next, the Warner management brought Brigitte Bardot into the house with the showing of the film "Female and the Flesh." It was definitely "Not Recommended for Children." And so the Warner, like most of the motion picture theatres of the time, succumbed to the R-rated picture in an attempt to keep the doors open.

Among the managers who had played a part in the success of this theatre during the years it operated were Alf B. Binnard, Helen Bortz, and Bert Leighton. But time ran out on March 14, 1963, when the Warner closed its doors forever after the evening showing of the film, "The Days of Wine and Roses," starring Jack Lemmon and Lee Remick. As an Eagle staff writer quipped, the film could well be retitled, "Days of Tears and Heartaches." The other theatre news that day was the announcement that the Loew's Theatre would also be closing when the lease with the Breneiser estate expired on March 31 of that year. However, the *Reading Eagle* article on March 14, which detailed the Warner's closing, noted that the Stanley Warner Corporation was negotiating to lease the former Loew's Colonial in hopes of reopening a theatre on the site. As described in the section relating the history of the Loew's, these negotiations were a success. Of course, the Warner eventually went the way of all Reading theatredom when it was torn down in the 70's to make way for the future Penn Street Mall. The site is now a parking lot.

Reading Eagle ad of December 27, 1958.

The first CinemaScope film plays the Warner. *Reading Eagle* ad - January 21, 1954.

The Warner attempted to keep up with changing times by bringing in adult films. *Reading Eagle* - January 21, 1960.

Final Curtain for Theater

This is the last day of operation for the Warner Theater, 755 Penn St., management announced today. The Stanley Warner Corp., operator of the entertainment house, is reportedly negotiating for the Loew's Colonial Theater building, 651 Penn St., which is expected to close March 31. For Warner employes who have gotten their quit notices, the film, showing for the last day, could well be retitled "Days of Tears and Heartaches."—Eagle Photo.

Reading Eagle **coverage of the March 14, 1963, closing of the Warner Theatre.**

The Princess Theatre at 819 Penn Street which became the "new Arcadia" for a brief time after the closing of the original Arcadia at 734 Penn Street. Photo courtesy of John Glase.

The "new Arcadia" which became the Ritz Theatre in 1941. Photo courtesy of John Glase.

16. The Ritz

This small theatre, which once stood at 819 Penn Street, had various names over the years, including the Crescent, the Princess, and even the Arcadia for a short time after the original Arcadia theatre in the 700 block of Penn Street was replaced by the Astor. However, in 1941, the Wilmer and Vincent theatre chain gained control of the site, made extensive improvements, and reopened the building as the Ritz. On February 7 of that year, Gene Autry came riding into the Ritz in the motion picture, "Ridin' on a Rainbow," which celebrated the grand opening. According to Paul Glase's written recollections, Wilmer and Vincent spent approximately $30,000 to make the theatre more attractive to patrons. They also quickly reassured the public that they intended to continue the children's parties which had been a staple of the movie house under the former management.

Indeed, for many children of that decade, the Ritz became the place to be on a Saturday morning when tickets cost a dime and the show was an all-day affair. As the ad which appeared in Wilmer and Vincent's publication, *The Moviegoer*, illustrates, the program consisted of one or two feature films (usually westerns), a serial (or "chapter"), a two-reel comedy, two color cartoons, and a "frolic program with lots of prizes." The Ritz was the place downtown where Mom sent the kids to get them out of the way for awhile while she shopped or housecleaned or did the myriad of things that were part of the housewife's chores in those days. Some kids even packed a lunch in anticipation of the many hours of entertainment that awaited them in that little, dark moviewomb on Penn Street. In addition, children were encouraged during the war years to do their part by bringing scrap to the theatre "to help Uncle Sam and see a thrilling show at the same time." Sometimes the scrap could be exchanged for a movie ticket.

In 1944, the Ritz joined the Fabian circuit. It was now promoted as "The Down-Town Family Theatre" and continued with a double-feature program of family films like the Henry Aldrich series and Brenda Starr serials. Bugs Bunny cartoons and the latest newsreel were also immensely popular with

The Ritz Theatre opened on February 7, 1941, a day before Doris Day appeared in person on the stage of the Astor Theatre.
***Reading Eagle* - February 7, 1941.**

patrons. Also continuing to play on the screen were westerns like the Red Ryder series, starring "Wild Bill" Elliott as Red and Bobby Blake as Little Beaver. Later, Allan "Rocky" Lane would appear on the Ritz's screen as Red Ryder. But it was not just the youngsters who enjoyed the Ritz's fare, for many an adult, after finishing shopping in the numerous stores which then adorned Penn Street, would cap off a perfect day by plunking down 30¢ at the box office window for a ticket to the land of Hollywood make-believe. The Ritz gladly provided the experience.

Among the managers listed in the city directories over the years were Otto Kyger, Jack Van, and James Moyer. Earl Arnold is the last manager of record at this theatre which, unfortunately, closed its fancy glass doors on September 26, 1951. Ironically, the little movie house, which had opened in 1941 as the Ritz with a Gene Autry film, now closed with "The Hills of Utah," also starring Autry. Kid's tickets to see Gene Autry were still 10¢ but it was to be the last "kiddie show" at the theatre. In fact, with no official announcement, the Ritz locked its doors forever. In approximately 1956, the theatre was torn down. The site is now a parking lot.

Ad which appeared on page 4 of the Wilmer and Vincent Theatre chain's publication, *The Moviegoer* (week of August 4, 1943). The misspelling of "Boots" in the Ritz Theatre ad was intentional as this issue contained a "misspelled word" contest which awarded free movie tickets to the winners.

(Opposite) The Ritz Theatre at 819 Penn Street. Since the theatre did not open under that name until 1941, the film, "The Plainsman," must have been a re-release since it was originally released in 1937.
Photo courtesy of Ed Foley.

The Park and the Ritz team up to help the war effort.
Reading Eagle - January 9, 1943.

Typical Ritz Theatre programs in the 1940s and 1950s when westerns were still popular with the movie-going public. *Reading Eagle* - January 12, 1948, March 17, 1948 and December 20, 1950.

17. The Park

In 1925, when the Reading Lodge, No. 155, Loyal Order of Moose, decided that their meeting places at the Arcadia Theatre and the old Academy Hall on Penn Square were no longer large enough to accommodate them, they acquired the building at 1018 Penn Street from Samuel Deibert. Two years later, they bought the adjacent property at 1016 Penn from Adam Reiser, and, next, acquired the properties at 1020 and 1022 from the Breneiser Estate. Here they built the Moose Temple. Over the years, the site has also housed the Park Luncheonette and its basement bowling alley, the Daniel Boone Hotel, the Coconut Grove nightclub and the Park Theatre.

The theatre opened on November 11, 1926, with the film, "Her Big Night," starring Laura La Plante, along with a program of vaudeville. Matinee prices were 15¢ for children and 25¢ for adults. Evening prices were higher. Patrons also heard a special musical performance by the Park Theatre Orchestra, under the direction of George Brensinger, and an organ recital by Margaret Gibney James. A few years later, Henry Brunner became the orchestra director while Mabel Stoudt and Ted Aurand performed at the console. Installed as resident manager was C.G. Keeney, assisted by Michael Stoltz. Paul Glase writes that the Penn Amusement

Notice of discontinuance of Sunday vaudeville programs at the Park Theatre as it appeared in the January 30, 1932, issue of the *Reading Eagle.*

(Opposite) The Park Theatre at 1016 Penn Street, circa late 1940's.
Photo courtesy of Ed Foley of Kenhorst.

To the Citizens of Reading:—

The management of the Park Theatre announces with the deepest regret that after Friday, February 12, we are discontinuing our policy of high-grade vaudeville.

Owing to the arbitrary discrimination against us on the part of the city authorities, we are unable to continue to offer the high quality of stage attractions that have been shown at the Park Theatre, and rather than become embroiled in an issue that might result in depriving the good people of Reading of Sunday baseball and other kindred amusements, to which they have been accustomed, although prohibited by a law passed 140 years ago under vastly different conditions of life, we have decided, despite heavy monetary loss, to discontinue vaudeville and change our policy to high-grade motion pictures only. We wish, at this time, to thank you fair-minded people of Reading for your many kindnesses to us, and trust that we may continue to merit your patronage in the future.

PARK THEATRE MANAGEMENT

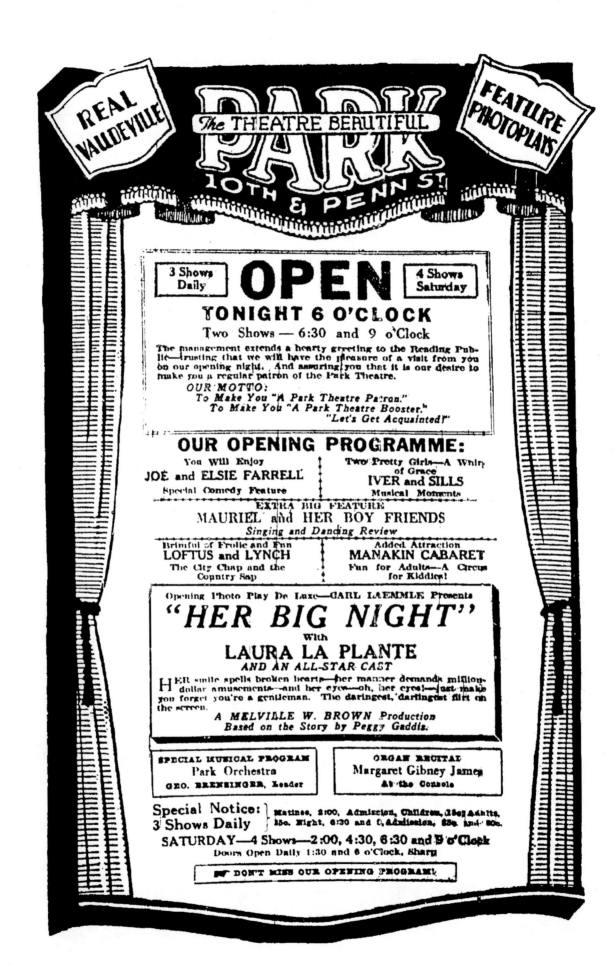

Company acted as promoters, naming Irving Goldstein as general manager. A *Reading Eagle* staff writer declared upon the opening of the Park on that Armistice Day that "the beauty of the place will be a surprise."

In his series of articles written for the *Historical Review of Berks County*, and later published in a special edition for friends and family, Paul E. Glase relates a brief history of this theatre, noting that, in 1929, the Park was equipped for sound before being taken over in 1931 by the United Theatre chain which renovated the fairly new movie house. However, in 1932, the theatre was temporarily closed by local authorities for staging vaudeville programs on Sundays, a closing the management did not take graciously. The Sunday evening benefits which the management had been staging since 1929, specifically for the Mooseheart Legion, were allowed to continue since there was no admission charge. Instead, donations were collected at the door. Taking their lead from the Park, other downtown movie houses began staging benefits for various organizations like the Veterans of Foreign Wars, Disabled Vets, American Legion Posts, and other community groups.

By 1933, the theatre was in the hands of the Reading National Bank. Fortunately, in 1936, the East Reading Theatre Company, with C.G. Keeney as president and Jay Emanuel as secretary, purchased the entertainment house. Keeney would continue at the helm until 1946 when he withdrew his interest in order to take over the lease of the Rajah Theatre and, later, the Orpheum which he renamed the Plaza. Under Keeney's management, the Park was a success. An April 17, 1939, article in the *Reading Eagle* revealed Keeney's generosity by noting that five hundred youngsters, including *Reading Times* carriers, children from orphanages, the Children's Home, and the Boy's Home, were treated to a free preview of the Fred Astaire and Ginger Roger's film, "The Story of Vernon and Irene Castle." In addition, each child was given oranges and apples as well as a free bus ride to and from the Park. The Park also hosted a film premiere that year when it was selected to be one of the first motion picture houses to show the film, "The Hunchback of Notre Dame," starring Charles Laughton and Maureen O'Hara. As the *Reading Eagle* ad of December 19, 1939, heralded, Reading

Reading Eagle ad of December 19, 1939, heralding the world premiere in Reading of "The Hunchback of Notre Dame."

(Opposite) Reading Eagle ad of November 11, 1926.

was "again highly honored by RKO, Radio Pictures for being selected for a world premiere ahead of Radio City Music Hall." Of course, as mentioned previously in the section detailing the Loew's Theatre, Reading had also been selected to premiere "Gone With the Wind."

Keeney's reign at this Reading theatre was not without its controversy, however. In 1940, a film entitled "The Ramparts We Watch" was released in America. Since the last reel of the film was made in Germany, the United States government felt that it was German propaganda against American ideals and customs. They proceeded to ban the film in this country. Mr. Keeney defied the ban and featured the film on September 18, 1940, at the Park. On September 19, the authorities closed the theatre. A new motion picture opened at the Park the next day.

Sometime during the fifties, the Fabian-Goldman chain took over the Park, appointing Emmanuel Rosenberg as manager. In 1958, the theatre closed again when its owners claimed that they could not operate profitably because of the city's 10% levy on gross receipts. Again, the shutdown was shortlived, for a few days after Christmas of that year, the Park reopened with a Bridgette Bardot film.

James Maurer took over the theatre around 1960, continuing to bring in the latest in movies and entertainment. An ad in the January 20, 1963, edition of the *Eagle* illustrated Maurer's attempt to bring back stage and screen shows by featuring the Glenn Miller Orchestra, under the direction of Ray McKinley, on stage and the motion picture, "The Glenn Miller Story," on the screen. Unfortunately, the audiences were no longer there so the Park moved from family fare to more adult entertainment like live burlesque and X-rated films.

The passing of the Park occurred on May 20, 1978, when the *Eagle* headlines spread the news that "Fire Destroys Park Theatre." The article detailing the fire was written by Richard Auman who told of the evacuation of eight persons from the Daniel Boone Hotel before the arrival on the scene by firemen at 3:18 A.M. Auman stated that the fire was confined mostly to the auditorium and the ceiling where some small fires burned. The stage area, however, sustained mostly water and smoke damage as its fireproof curtains saved it from destruction by flames. Auman noted that Maurer had been planning to close the movie house before the city had a chance to shut it down for 273 Code violations. Now there was no need to take such action. What had once been a promising showplace became a pile of rubble as, four days after the fire, the City of Reading ordered the Park Theatre and portions of the Daniel Boone Hotel demolished. It is now an empty lot.

James Maurer attempts to bring back stage and screen programs to the Park Theatre.
Reading Eagle ad of January 20, 1963.

SITE OF BLAZE — Hose from city fire companies, bottom photo, snakes through city streets to the site of the Park Theater on Penn Street, which was gutted by fire early this morning. The fire was mostly confined to the auditorium of the theater, however, there also were small fires in the ceiling areas of the Daniel Boone Hotel which abuts the theater. — Eagle Photos by Owen C. Stout.

Reading Eagle coverage of the May 20, 1978, fire which destroyed the Park and damaged the Daniel Boone Hotel.

WET LOUNGE — The lounge of the Park Theater sustained extensive water damage but the fire was confined to the main auditorium of the theater. The fire also caused damage to the rear section of the Daniel Boone Hotel. — Eagle Photo by Owen C. Stout.

Fire Guts Theater; Hotel Is Evacuated

18. The Astor

In 1891, the Keystone Market House at 734 Penn Street was transformed into the Eden Musée (a curio hall and museum) and the Bijou Theatre. As Paul Glase recalls, the property underwent various name changes over the next twenty-five years, including Gilder's Auditorium, Becker's Lyceum, the "New Bijou," and the Palace. Then, on June 26, 1916, Carr and Schad purchased the site, remodeled the building, and reopened it as the "New Arcadia," featuring motion pictures and musical programs, with a house orchestra under the direction of Harry E. Fahrbach, accompanied by the Kimball organ. Musical scores were especially arranged for the attractions on the screen. In 1920, a four-manual Moller organ was installed for the listening pleasure of Readingites who made the Arcadia a success for the Carr and Schad enterprise. In fact, the theatre was successful for twelve years until an announcement was made in the May 28, 1928, edition of the *Reading Eagle* that a new theatre, the Astor, would be opening on the site of the Arcadia. Thus, after a two-day farewell program, which featured the motion picture, "Honor Bound," with George O'Brien, a song and organ specialty number with Howard (Hops) Heinly singing "Bye Gone Days," and a rhyming story detailing the history of the Arcadia, the theatre closed on May 30, 1928. In its place would come the Franklin Theatre Company's newest picture house, the Astor Theatre, which the local newspaper described as "one of the finest houses of amusement of its kind in this section of the state."

Advance newspaper publicity on April 8, 1928, heralded the building's planned architectural features. It was designed by William H. Lee, one of the best-known theatrical architects in the country. C.H. Schlegel of Reading was in charge of construction for the Astor which would be built of terra cotta in the modern French design. The entire theatre was to be fireproof, with a proposed seating capacity of three thousand (two thousand on the first floor and a thousand in the balcony). The entrance and vestibule would remain in the same location as the present entrance to the Arcadia. Large, open, marble-tread stairways with ornamental iron rails would lead to the mezzanine floor and balcony. Lounges, desks, reading tables, public telephones, and other amenities for the convenience of the patrons were to be located on the mezzanine floor, with marble and tile drinking fountains mirrored in the walls.

The projection booth, containing four projection machines and Vitaphone apparatus, was to be the largest of its kind in any theatre in the state, according to the staff writer for the *Eagle*. The stage would display the latest in modern grid iron and dressing rooms while being able to accommodate vaudeville,

The Arcadia Theatre at 734 Penn Street, later to become the Astor. Photo courtesy of John Glase.

(Opposite) Newspaper ad for the "Gala Opening" of the Astor Theatre on October 3, 1928.

musical comedy, opera, and dramatic productions. The $25,000 disappearing orchestra pit, which was compared to those in the Roxy Theatre in New York and Grauman's in Hollywood, was planned so as to be capable of carrying more than twenty-five musicians to three levels of the theatre: the basement, which was connected to the orchestra room; the stage level, for overtures and presentations; and the floor level, for motion pictures. Moreover, the orchestra lift, as well as the independent lift for the $40,000 four-manual Wurlitzer pipe organ, could be operated by the orchestra conductor by a touch of the button. Other attributes included heavy, upholstered, steel chairs with real tapestry and concealed aisle lights.

The furniture in the lobby, mezzanine, retiring, and men's smoking rooms was to be styled after the massive French design. The second floor would contain the offices of the Franklin Company with a private projection room and a soundproof studio broadcasting room. The exterior of the building, constructed of terra cotta with a marble base, would feature a large marquee and vertical sign spelling out the name of the theatre in thousands of electric light bulbs with changeable colors operating continuously. New vacuum tube lighting was planned for the illumination of the windows and arches.

On the evening of October 3, 1928, three thousand people filled this newest, art deco theatre to hear Walter Marshall, the leading man of the Orpheum Players, read the prologue, "Let There Be Light." Glase recalls in his articles that as the orchestra of sixteen musicians, under the direction of Vincent Kay, played "The Star-Spangled Banner," the "Goddess of Light" appeared and the show began. The feature motion picture that evening was "Street Angel," with Janet Gaynor and Charles Farrell, while the stage presentation consisted of the "Circus Follies." Of course, before the program began, local dignitaries made a few speeches, including one by Oliver M. Wolfe, the district attorney and master of ceremonies,

The early days of the Astor Theatre at 734 Penn Street which opened on October 3, 1928. This photo shows the first marquee.
Photo courtesy of John Glase.

Usher inspection behind the Astor Theatre.
Photo courtesy of John Glase.

who remarked, "We can scarcely realize when we glance around this theatre that we are on Penn Street and not on Broadway."

Two years later, on June 30, 1930, the Warner Company took over the Astor, along with the Strand and the balance of the old Franklin circuit. The new management continued the practice of presenting both motion pictures and stage acts. It was during their eleven-year reign that Hoot Gibson, Edgar Bergen, Abbott and Costello, and the Les Brown Orchestra, featuring Doris Day as vocalist, appeared on the stage. Also notable is the fact that Paul Glase, who had been the general manager for the Franklin Chain, continued in the same capacity for the Warner operation for approximately two years at which time he joined the Wilmer and Vincent theatrical chain. Assisting Glase were Clarence Latshaw as house manager and Earl Westbrooke as assistant manager.

After the Warner lease expired in 1941, the Astor closed for renovations, reopening on May 28, 1941, as a Schad theatre under the partnership of Harry J. and Sallie Schad. Renovations included a new marquee, new seats and carpeting. In 1946, the operating company was changed to a corporation known as Schad Theatres, Inc., with H.J. Schad as president, Sallie Schad as vice-president, and Louise Esterly as secretary-treasurer. According to Glase, when Mrs. Schad died, Paul Esterly became the vice-president of the corporation. Also at this time, J. Lester Stallman became associated with the Astor as city

Reading Eagle ad for February 8, 1941.

Reading Eagle ad for September 15, 1943.

**The reopening of the Astor Theatre by new manager, Harry J. Schad, on May 28, 1941.
Schad's renovations included a new marquee.
Photo courtesy of the late Richard Houck.**

Reading Eagle ad for April 12, 1952, when Abbott and Costello appeared on the stage of the Astor.

representative, an association which would last for more than twenty years.

Like the rest of Reading's theatre managers, Stallman contributed his services to the numerous bond rallies held in the city. As mentioned previously, the managers marshalled parades, directed mass meetings and scrap drives, and staged War Bond premieres with free shows for those buying bonds. In fact, these theatre operators promoted the sale of over five million dollars in War Bonds, bringing to Reading such famous stars of the time as Ray Bolger, John Garfield, Paulette Goddard, and Patsy Kelly to aid in their selling efforts. One War Bond event at the Astor featured Fred Astaire and Joan Leslie on screen in "The Sky's the Limit" and the Johhny Weiss Orchestra entertaining on the stage. Anyone buying a War Bond received a free ticket to the show. Of course, some promotions were aimed at keeping the crowds coming to the downtown movie houses. One such event was the essay contest which appeared in the Astor's movie ad in the December 21, 1943, issue of the *Reading Eagle*. The title of the 100 word essay was "Why I Would Like to Meet Frank Sinatra" and its grand prize was a trip to Philadelphia to have lunch with the popular crooner. Also included was the chance to be photographed "swooning" beside "the Voice."

Lester Stallman continued the Astor policy of film and stage presentations into the fifties, as seen by the appearance of Bud Abbott and Lou Costello on April 12, 1952, in a promotion for their latest film, "Jack and the Beanstalk." CinemaScope also came to the Astor during the fifties with motion pictures like "How to Marry a Millionaire," starring Marilyn Monroe, Betty Grable, and Lauren Bacall. Another promotional tool was the "midnite show" featuring "one showing only" of a new Hollywood film for the ticket price of 70¢. But the Astor was to change hands again, for on April 30, 1956, the *Eagle* carried the news that William Goldman Theatres, Inc. of Philadelphia would be taking over the leases for the Astor and the Strand from the Schad Corporation.

Along with the new management came extensive renovations, among them a new marquee, a new neon-illuminated, upright sign, and a new building facade. The lobby was also redecorated, new doors were installed, and the box office was moved from the center to the west side of the building. J. Lester Stallman was to remain as city district supervisor, while Clayton Evans would hold the same position at the Strand. The new Goldman 2,150 seat Astor would continue to provide wholesome entertainment for Reading's moviegoers for the next sixteen years, although films such as "Peyton

Reading Eagle ad for January 8, 1954.

(Opposite) The Astor Theatre, circa 1941, the year that the second marquee was installed. The film, "The Gold Rush," which was originally released in 1924, was re-released in 1941.
Photo courtesy of Ron Romanski.

114

Reading Eagle ad for the Astor's "Giant Scream Show" held on March 1, 1963. Note that free 45 RPM records were given to the first 300 patrons.

Place" in 1959 and "Return to Peyton Place" in 1961 foreshadowed the "adults only" films which were destined to take over movie houses all over the country. However, during the late fifties and early sixties, patrons still bought tickets to the family films like Disney's "Pollyanna" in 1960 and "The Absent-Minded Professor" in 1961. In fact, Disney films never seemed to lose their popularity. When "101 Dalmations" played the Astor in 1969, the management ran a contest awarding a live Dalmation puppy "to some lucky boy or girl." Besides contests, the Astor used other promotional tools to attract patrons during these years. The events which probably drew the most crowds were the "Scream Shows" like the one which was featured on March 1, 1963, which boasted of an appearance on stage by the Frankenstein Monster and Dracula, "direct from Hollywood, in person and alive." Those brave enough to attend the show were warned to be prepared to experience the "Horrors of the Living Dead" as Dracula flew into the audience in the form of a bat. Those patrons who did not run screaming from the theatre but remained in their seats after these terrifying events were rewarded with two horror films to keep the fear alive. At some of these shows, a nurse was on duty to assist those who might faint from fright. And if all of these scary events were not enough to entice an audience, the management extended an extra bonus by giving free 45 RPM records to the first three hundred patrons. Best of all, the price for a ticket to this magnificent horrorland was a mere one dollar bill!

Along with porn movies, the 70's brought hard times to the Astor. In 1971, the house organ was sold, and in 1972, the Reading Redevelopment Authority acquired the old movie house for $310,000, leasing it to the Fox Theatre Management which ran it until 1975 when it closed as a film venue. An article in the December 10 edition of the *Eagle* that year stated that the cost factor for running the theatre was the reason for the closing. Apparently, according to the staff writer for the local paper, the RRA could not meet the tax bill of $12,000 without increasing the rent for Fox. However, Fox could not afford the increase since business was slowing down while heating costs were soaring in a building whose furnace was eating up five tons of coal per week. Therefore, the "stalwart vestige of Reading's old glory," as the *Eagle* writer tagged it, would no longer be home to the motion picture. However, no indication was given that the RRA planned to raze it. Rather, it seemed that they were seriously considering the costs involved in repairing the roof and the heating system in order to lease out the building as a private facility.

In an article which appeared in the September 18, 1987, issue of the *Reading Times*, entitled "Astor's Elegance Is Remembered," writer Stephanie Ebberts recalls that the Penn Square Commission leased the Astor building in 1976 from the RRA, entering into an agreement with Gavin Productions to sponsor live concerts on the Astor stage. Among the entertainers who appeared at these events were Barry Manilow, Bonnie Raitt, and Billy Joel, with crowds ranging from 1,250 to a sold-out house of 2,400 patrons. Sadly, by the end of the seventies, even the concerts were gone. Optimistically, some supporters of the theatre succeeded in having the Astor placed on the National Register of Historic Places in 1976 to prevent its demolition. Later, in the eighties, "The Friends of the Astor," a group founded by businessman Louis Perugini, attempted to raise funds and build support for restoring the theatre, but without success. Perugini, however, did manage to have some repairs made to the building, particularly the roof, to prevent major structural damage, and has continued to fight over the years for the restoration of this art deco masterpiece.

Various nostalgic articles have been written about the Astor over the last twenty years. In addition to the aforementioned article of September 18, 1987, Ms. Ebberts also published an interview with former employee, Charles Hill, in that same issue of the *Times*. The article, entitled "Employee Reminisces About Theatre's Glory Days," told of Hill's memories of the Astor during the twenty-five years of his employment there. Hill recalled that he began his theatre career on January 1, 1946, on the day that the motion picture, "The Bells of St. Mary's," starring Bing Crosby, opened at the movie house. Later,

The bugles blare for the 1962 film, "Hell is for Heroes." This marquee, the third for the theatre, was installed in 1956.
Photo courtesy of the late Richard Houck.

INTERIOR PHOTOS OF THE ASTOR THEATRE

These photos were taken sometime in the 1970's in conjuction with a feasibility study. Courtesy of the Reading Redevelopment Authority.

A view of the large mirrors and art deco design in the lobby.

The auditorium with a view of the balcony.

The lobby of the Astor. In lower left-hand corner is the candy counter

The entrance to the seating area downstairs.

The mezzanine floor, right-hand side.

A section of the balcony showing one of the beautiful art deco sunbursts.

The mezzanine floor on the left side of the theatre. Note the tiled drinking fountain on the right.

Looking down from the balcony to the stage.

working as a doorman and maintenance man, Mr. Hill met many entertainers who appeared at the Astor. Among these were Boris Karloff, Bob Hope, Van Heflin, and Abbott and Costello. This former Astor employee remembered that lowering the one-half ton glass chandelier with its 109 light bulbs for cleaning was a two-man job. And when the job was accomplished, the huge lighting fixture covered five rows of seats! At Christmas, Hill would put up a tree in the lobby and decorate it with florescent balls, putting black lights above it. The lobby chandelier would be decorated with red and green lights. The former theatre man also recalled the painted stage curtain with its scene of Hampden Boulevard with the Pagoda in the background. When Hill returned to the old theatre in 1987, he was heartbroken over its condition for it was so beautiful when he worked there. In the article, Hill states that he just can't forget the Astor and still has dreams that he's back in its splendor, working the aisles again.

Donald Mellinger also has fond memories of shows at the Astor. Mellinger remembers well the man in the Frankenstein Monster suit who came into the audience to promote the coming attraction featuring the creature. Moreover, he can still hear in his memory the music of the dance band that played in the theatre's mezzanine to promote the film, "42nd Street."

Everyone has different memories of the Astor. For some, it's a leisurely window-shopping stroll up Penn Street on a sunny Easter afternoon on the way to see Disney's "Cinderella." Or standing in the crowd outside the box office listening to the blare of the brass horns which played for the opening of "Hell is for Heroes." Others remember watching the ever-smiling contestants for the "Miss Reading Fair" crown as they strutted down the runway jutting out from the Astor's stage in their bid for local fame. RHS alumni recall the lively pep rallies and the athletic parties held at the art deco movie house. And who can ever forget the smell of the Crystal Palace next store where the man stacked luscious hot dogs up his arm for theatregoers who sat at one-armed chairs to eat such delicacies?

In September of 1994, the *Reading Eagle* news staff wrote an article for the paper entitled "Time Hasn't Been Kind to the Astor," a story which detailed the theatre's bygone splendor and quoted a 1928 opening night item which appeared in the local paper. The scribes of 1928 had reported that the most outstanding elements of the art deco style in the new movie house were two wall decorations in the shape of "superbly proportioned sunbursts... silhouetted in front of a large niche lighted from below by a myriad of colors. In the center of each sunburst is a large jewel-shaped lighting fixture which twinkles and gleams during the picture." That same opening night article described the water fountains as "laid up in a way that suggests a modern skyscraper," a design typical of the art deco style. Indeed, Newton A. Perrin, Ph.D., claimed in a June 17, 1987, *Reading Times* story, "Astor Theatre is Art Deco Masterpiece," that the Astor may be one of the oldest surviving examples of theatre art deco in the United States.

As of this writing, the Astor Theatre still stands. Incredibly, many of her treasures remain inside her weather-beaten, roof-leaking frame. Undeniably, her art deco splendor, once sparkling with gold leaf and myriads of color, is now, after twenty years of neglect, chipped and waterstained, her plaster crumbling from too much Reading rain and her floors becoming littered with greywhite pigeon droppings. But, unlike the rest of the Penn Street movie theatres, the Astor has managed to woo a few suitors. And, so she stands, refusing to give up her hope chest. Presently, attempts are being made to demolish the old theatre to make way for a brand new venue of entertainment - a civic center. However, nothing they build can ever replace the art deco splendor of the Astor Theatre.

THE END

Sources

Adams, Charles J., III, *Ghost Stories of Berks County - Book Two*, Reading, Exeter House Books, 1984.

"Astor is Closed As Movie House," *Reading Eagle*, December 10, 1975.

Auman, Richard D., "Fire Destroys Park Theatre," *Reading Eagle*, May 20, 1978.

——"Theatre's History Stormy," *Reading Eagle*, May 20, 1978.

"Capitol Sold," *Reading Eagle*, October 3, 1925.

"Capitol Theatre Opens Thursday Afternoon," *Reading Eagle*, September 4, 1921.

Ebbert, Stephanie, "Astor's Elegance Is Remembered," *Reading Times*, September 8, 1987.

—— "Employee Reminisces About Theatre's Glory Days," *Reading Times*, September 8, 1987.

"Embassy Theatre Opens Today," *Reading Eagle*, April 4, 1931.

"Farewell Program at Arcadia," *Reading Eagle*, May 28, 1928.

Gallagher, Charles M., "Fire Damages Strand Theatre," *Reading Eagle*, February 23, 1970.

—— "Fire Wrecks Embassy Theatre," *Reading Eagle*, March 16, 1970.

Glase, Paul E., "Annals of the Reading Stage: Early Theatre and Playbills -- 1873-1917," *Historical Review of Berks County*, Vol. 11, No. 3, pp. 75-84, April, 1947.

—— "Annals of the Reading Stage: Early Theatre and Playbills -- 1891-1947," *Historical Review of Berks County*, Vol. 12, No. 4, pp. 107-115, July, 1947.

——"The Motion Picture Theatre in Reading: Silent Drama Days -- 1905-1926," *Historical Review of Berks County*, Vol. 13, No. 2, pp. 35-44, January, 1948.

——"The Motion Picture Theatre in Reading: The Start of Talking Pictures -- 1927-1948," *Historical Review of Berks County*, Vol. 13, No. 3, pp. 79-88, April, 1948.

—— *Annals of the Reading Theatre -- 1791-1948* (compilation of articles published in the *Historical Review of Berks County*), Reading, 1948.

—— Scrapbook Number 4, Historical Society of Berks County Archives.

"Half Million Dollar Astor Theatre to Open Next October on Arcadia Site," *Reading Eagle*, April 8, 1928.

"Loew's Closes, Will Reopen Under New Name," *Reading Eagle*, April 1, 1963.

Lucia, Tony, "A Movie Palace Crumbles," *Reading Eagle*, February 19, 1984.

Meiser, George M., IX, and Gloria Jean Meiser, *The Passing Scene - Volume 8*, Reading, Reading Eagle Press, 1992.

Meiser, George M., IX, "Penn Street Theatres," *Historical Review of Berks County*, Vol. 42, No. 3, pp. 100-101, Summer, 1977.

Moser, Nick, "Plank Will Bid Farewell to Embassy Theatre Tonight," *Reading Eagle*, March 31, 1970.

The Moviegoer, Wilmer and Vincent publication, Vol. 4, No. 10, August 4, 1943.

"Pauline Frederick to Open New Theatre on Monday," *Reading Eagle*, April 15, 1917.

Perrin, Newton A., Ph. D., "Astor Theatre Is Art Deco Masterpiece," *Reading Times*, June 17, 1987.

Peters, Dick, "Cowboy Hero Here to Stay, Autry Tells Small Fry," *Reading Times*, February 19, 1954.

Reading Newsweek - Volume 1, Reading, Reading Eagle Press, 1992.

Reading Newsweek - Volume 2, Reading, Reading Eagle Press, 1993.

Shirey, Shirley, "Reading's Old-Time Picture Houses Revisited," *Berks County Record*, April 4, 1968.

"State's Opening Draws Capacity Crowds," *Reading Eagle*, October 11, 1925.

"Time Hasn't Been Kind to the Astor," *Reading Eagle*, September 4, 1994.

Tobias, Joseph J., "Film Projectionists Recall the Early Talkies Here," *Sunday Eagle Magazine*, August 20, 1961.

"Warner Closes Tonight; Officials Change Minds," *Reading Eagle*, March 14, 1963.